END

Because of Dennis and Dr. Jen Clarks' teaching I can walk in supernatural peace 24/7.

SID ROTH
host, *It's Supernatural!*

Few aspects of the Christian life are as important, misunderstood, or underutilized as the incredible power of God's peace. Too often, we view peace merely as a pleasant feeling rather than what it really is—a mighty river of God's healing grace and provision. In *The Supernatural Power of Peace*, Dennis and Dr. Jen Clark introduce you to a life of deeper peace than you've ever experienced before, filled with the Prince of Peace Himself.

JIM BUCHAN
Crosslink Ministries

The Supernatural Power of Peace is written by a couple who live in the Peace of God daily, living what they preach. This is not theory. This not something written about a few people or a few hundred people ministered to. This is written by two people who live this every day and have been living it for years. If you do not walk in the fullness of the peace of the Lord, you will, by reading this carefully and practicing the things that are taught here, know that your life will be transformed so that you too will be able to say that you walk in the peace of the Lord.

Dennis makes the following statement: "I have lived a lifestyle of communion with God long enough to prove to me that walking in peace is more reliable than any amount of logical information. If peace guides me, then I know I'm in God's will."

The Supernatural Power of Peace is valuable for everyone from the mature Christian to the unbeliever, although any unbeliever seriously reading this book will no longer be an unbeliever. I heartily recommend *The Supernatural Power of Peace*.

REV. WILLIAM J. MORFORD
author/translator of the *One New Man Bible*

THE
SUPER
NATURAL
POWER
OF
PEACE

DESTINY IMAGE BOOKS BY
DENNIS AND DR. JEN CLARK

Live Free

Deep Relief Now

THE SUPER NATURAL POWER OF PEACE

DENNIS *and*
DR. JEN CLARK

DESTINY IMAGE® PUBLISHERS, INC.
P.O. Box 310, Shippensburg, PA 17257-0310
"Promoting Inspired Lives."

This book and all other Destiny Image and Destiny Image Fiction books are available at Christian bookstores and distributors worldwide.

Cover and interior design by: Terry Clifton

For more information on foreign distributors, call 717-532-3040.
Reach us on the Internet: www.destinyimage.com.

ISBN 13 TP: 978-0-7684-0533-0
ISBN 13 Ebook: 978-0-7684-0534-7

For Worldwide Distribution, Printed in the U.S.A.
1 2 3 4 5 6 7 8 / 19 18 17 16 15

DEDICATION

We dedicate this book to our son, Jason Clark. Thank you for your prayers, confirming revelations from God, being a watchman on the wall, and building our computers, as well as providing tech support and the artistry of your video editing. We greatly appreciate your integrity, pureness of heart, and wisdom that is far beyond your years. There are many godly young men in the body of Christ, but you are truly exemplary. If we wrote out a "wish list" for the qualities of an ideal son, disciple, and pastor you would exceed our hopes and dreams. Thank you most of all for becoming a living epistle of all we teach in this book. You, like David, are truly "a man after God's own heart."

ACKNOWLEDGMENTS

We are deeply grateful for all those who made this book possible and wish to personally thank the following people for their contributions and support: Thank you, Destiny Image Publishers, for your vision and your obedience to the Lord. Without you this book would not have been written. We especially thank Ronda Ranalli, Director of Author Acquisitions and Production, for being the catalyst. We would also like to thank our editor, Ryan Adair. Thank you for your assistance in planning and editing this book. It has been a pleasure working with you. For all your proofreading, literary suggestions, and general support, we especially express our appreciation to Rebecca Lebovich. You will never know how highly we value your assistance. We also offer special thanks to our pastoral team for your input, support, and prayers. Thank you, Jason Clark, Senior Associate Pastor, and Associate Pastors Cliff and Stina Coon, Vicky Rose, and Molly Tarr.

CONTENTS

PREFACE

By Dr. Jen

Although *The Supernatural Power of Peace* covers many topics about the peace of God, Dennis and I endeavor throughout this book to teach you *how to make Jesus Christ Lord* of your life in a very practical way. When Jesus is Lord of our life, we can experience the gift of peace He gave us at every moment of every day. If He is the One who *gave* us His peace, then it should always be available for us (see John 14:27). Therefore, why does supernatural peace seem to be such an elusive experience for most Christians?

The answer is quite simple. Many believers have not been taught how to yield to the peace of God in everyday life, even though the Bible clearly exhorts us to *"let the peace of God rule"* in our hearts (Col. 3:15). The Lord certainly doesn't tell us to do something without giving us the ability and grace to obey Him (see Ps. 40:6 AMP).

Many Christians know Jesus as their Savior but still continue to live mostly for themselves. They pose little, if any, threat to the enemy. However, the devil greatly fears those believers who completely surrender to Jesus, making Him Lord of all. The Scriptures clearly reveal that nobody can say, "Jesus is Lord," *except* by the Holy Spirit. And no *evil spirit* would ever want believers to submit more completely to the lordship of Jesus Christ.

> *Therefore I tell you that no one who is speaking by the Spirit of God says, "Jesus be cursed," and no one can say, "Jesus is Lord," except by the Holy Spirit* (1 Corinthians 12:3 NIV).

For those of us who seek to know Him as Lord, the question then becomes, "How do I make Him Lord of my life?" We know we *should* live under the lordship of Jesus Christ, and in order for that to happen the Spirit must rule. What is the evidence of Spirit rule? At any given moment, when the Holy Spirit rules us, we have peace on the inside. Likewise, whenever the Holy Spirit is not ruling, we don't have peace. When we lose our peace, it is always possible to regain it by submitting to the lordship of Jesus Christ.

We can't just decide to be "good people" and try to live by the Golden Rule (see Luke 6:31). No one can read their Bible and obey all of it in the power of the flesh. If we could live by God's standards without Him, we wouldn't need Him. We can meet the requirements of God only by the grace that He gives to us.

What is grace? The reality of grace encompasses much more than that which is expressed by the definition "unmerited favor." *Vine's Expository Dictionary of Old and New Testament*

Words says grace includes "the power and equipment for ministry, e.g. Rom. 1:5, 12:6; 15:5; 1 Cor. 3:10; Gal. 2:9; Eph. 3:2, 7."[1] Grace is, therefore, the personal presence of Jesus living His life in us and through us by the power of the Holy Spirit (see Gal. 2:20-21). John tells us that grace comes from the fullness of Christ (see John 1:16), so grace is greater than unmerited favor. Through grace, God responds to our need and makes His power available to us.[2]

Left to our own resources, we are spiritually bankrupt. It is impossible for any good thing to come from our flesh. God created us as thinking, willing, feeling beings. It is clear that, even though we may be Christians, we can still have impure thoughts, make bad choices, and have carnal emotions. We must choose between flesh and Spirit. Even so-called good deeds, when motivated by the flesh, still have a wrong source. The Bible calls them "dead works" (see Heb. 6:1). Only that which comes from the Spirit has life. Jesus said, *"It is the Spirit who gives life; the flesh profits nothing"* (John 6:63).

Jesus can truly be Lord of our life only when we come to Him, admit our inability to meet His standards apart from Him, and surrender to His lordship. Knowing biblical information about God is not enough. Jesus rebuked the Pharisees because they studied the Scriptures most diligently but did not come to Jesus for life.

> *You search the Scriptures, for in them you think you have eternal life; and these are they which testify of Me. But you are not willing to come to Me that you may have life* (John 5:39-40).

We cannot read the Bible and then do what it says in our own strength or by our own willpower. If it wasn't possible to keep the law under the Old Covenant, then how can we live up to the higher standards set by Jesus under the New Covenant? We must be empowered by the life of God. We shouldn't "come to Jesus" only once when we get saved and then live in the flesh thereafter. We must continually come to Him and abide in His supernatural life (see John 15:5).

How does Jesus give us life? It can only come through the power of the Holy Spirit. We can do nothing in and of ourselves but live in carnality (see 2 Cor. 3:5-6). We are only able to live by the life of God when we walk in the Spirit of God. This is why Paul said, *"I say then: Walk in the Spirit, and you shall not fulfill the lust of the flesh"* (Gal. 5:16).

The lordship of Jesus Christ and our surrender to Him is foundational to New Testament revelation. We were made to serve Him, not ourselves. Let us come to Him so the Holy Spirit can teach us how to live under the lordship of Jesus Christ in the supernatural power of peace. As we yield to Him in this way, may Paul's words ring true:

> *That at the name of Jesus every knee should bow, of those in heaven, and of those on earth, and of those under the earth, and that every tongue should confess that Jesus Christ is Lord, to the glory of God the Father* (Philippians 2:10-11).

ENDNOTES

1.   *W. E. Vine, Vine's Expository Dictionary of Old and New Testament Words* (Old Tappan, NJ: Fleming H. Revell Company, Vol 4, 1981), 170.

2.   Footnote for John 1:16, from *The Spirit-Filled Life Bible,* ed. Jack Hayford (Nashville, TN: Thomas Nelson Publishers, 1991), 1574.

INTRODUCTION

BY DENNIS

ROOTED IN PEACE

An ominous sense of foreboding caused the hair to stand up on the back of my neck. Something real bad was up—I was sure of it. No one was doing anything that looked suspicious to the naked eye, but I had felt this feeling before. Every time someone planned to make a break for it or do something violent to another inmate, I could sense a buzz of negative energy, which was as disconcerting as being surrounded by a swarm of invisible bees.

I was a young Christian in my twenties, barely saved, and still "wet behind the ears," as they say. An old row house in a scary section of town had been adapted by a Christian ministry to be a halfway house for ex-convicts of all ages. Saved out of a life of drugs and alcohol and well acquainted with the roughest of the rough—having been brought up on the south side of Chicago and later working hardscrabble factory jobs—I figured this sort of work was my calling. I volunteered to work with the inmates to help out wherever I was needed and to generally keep an eye on things.

As the sun set and darkness fell, I knew we were in for it, whatever "it" was. Something fraught with danger was imminent. Suddenly, it happened! Fast as a bolt of lightning, a wild-eyed prisoner made a dash for the kitchen and grabbed a vicious-looking butcher knife, intending to make a break for it.

Weapon in hand, he bolted out the kitchen door, and there I was, standing directly in front of the exit door. He glared at me in rage and snarled, "Get out of my way or I'll cut you to pieces!" I didn't budge, but it wasn't because I was paralyzed with fear. Instead, as I stood there I felt completely surrounded by a strong sense of supernatural peace and had an inner certainty that the peace was impenetrable. Nothing could get past this peace to harm me—of that I was certain. So I stood and waited.

Sure enough, within moments I felt him soften. He didn't injure me or try to run. Instead, his hand started to tremble and shake. Abruptly, the knife clattered to the floor. Collapsing onto his knees, he began to cry. Peace proved to be a militant force in this frightening situation, empowering me to stand my ground while God worked on my behalf.

WHAT IS PEACE?

What is this *peace* that can calm a raging heart and create a bulwark against which the forces of darkness are impotent? Peace, in our modern Western thought, has been watered down to mean tranquility or freedom from war. Peace, however, is not passive or wimpy. It is not just the absence of conflict. On the contrary, peace is a mighty force, although it is little understood. For those who tap into the power of peace, it is life changing.

Peace is the power that enabled Jesus to walk through the crowd that sought to throw Him off of a cliff (see Luke 4:16-30), the energy in the Living Word that brought order out of chaos at the time of creation (see Gen. 1), and the authority to calm a stormy sea (see Mark 4:35-41). Peace is the force that holds the entire universe together (see Col. 1:16-17; Heb. 1:1-3). Peace forms the bonds that open a portal, which allows the glory of God to be poured out from heaven to earth (see Acts 2:2; 4:31; Eph. 4:3).

Peace is the essence of the kingdom of God. The kingdom of God is governed by peace. Wherever the peace of God advances, His kingdom is ordered and established. *"The kingdom of God is...righteousness and peace and joy in the Holy Spirit"* (Rom. 14:17). The government of God and His peace are inseparable. Isaiah prophesied:

> *And His name will be called Wonderful, Counselor, Mighty God, Everlasting Father, Prince of Peace. Of the increase of His government and peace there will be no end* (Isaiah 9:6-7).

Jesus gave us His own supernatural peace as a gift. His peace is not just calmness or absence of conflict. It is filled with power! Jesus promises us: *"Peace I leave with you, My peace I give to you; not as the world gives do I give to you. Let not your heart be troubled, neither let it be afraid"* (John 14:27).

When we walk in the peace that God gives, people or circumstances can't control us. Was Jesus ever frazzled or anxious? Of course not! He is the Prince of Peace. He has perfect peace, has authority to give us peace, and is the Commander of peace. From the place of peace, Jesus could sleep in the boat in the middle of a terrible storm, then stand and command the wind and waves, saying, *"Peace, be still!"* The One who spoke, "Elements align!" when the world was made still speaks today.

The same Prince of Peace who took authority over a storm on the Sea of Galilee also has authority over the storms of life. Romans 16:20 assures us, *"The God of peace will crush Satan under your feet shortly."* Peace is living in the presence of the Prince of Peace, for *"He Himself is our peace"* (Eph. 2:14). When we are in peace, we are in the presence of God. Peace is powerful. Peace is triumphant. Peace is victory!

The Hebrew word for *peace* is *shalom*. The *shalom* of God includes wholeness, peace, health and healing, welfare, safety, salvation, deliverance, soundness, prosperity, perfectness, fullness, rest, harmony, no injustice, and no pain. Peace is the *essence* of the elusive abundant life promised by Jesus!

HIS WILL IS LIKE A RIVER

The will of God is the expression of the perfection of heaven. It abounds with His life and love and glory. It accomplishes His purposes for the highest good. The inhabitants of heaven continuously rejoice as God's will is done.

God's will is released in a river of shalom. Everywhere shalom flows, there the kingdom of God is established. Just as chaos was conquered by peace when the worlds were created, shalom still triumphs today. The river of peace flows from Genesis to Revelation and down through the ages (see Gen. 2:10; Rev. 22:1-2).

The Book of Isaiah uses the word *shalom* 27 times, which is more than any other book in the Bible. The subject of peace begins with the Prince of Peace and His ever-increasing government in Isaiah 9:6-7, and it concludes with God's promise to *"extend peace...like a river"* (Isa. 66:12). *Extend* is the Hebrew word *natâh*, meaning to stretch, extend, expand. According to *New Wilson's Old Testament Word Studies*, "I will extend peace like a river" means *in the abundance and perpetuity of a full large river.*[1]

Shalom brings peace not only to individual hearts but in the nations of the earth as well. Isaiah tells us that a day will come when violence will end and men will *"beat their swords into plowshares, and their spears into pruning hooks; nation shall not lift up sword against nation, neither shall they learn war anymore"* (Isa. 2:1-4).

The Book of Daniel announces that someday a rock cut out of a mountain without hands will expand and fill the whole earth with the kingdom of God (see Dan. 2:31-44). *"And in the days of these kings the God of heaven will set up a kingdom which shall never be destroyed; and the kingdom shall not be left to other people; it shall break in pieces and consume all these kingdoms, and it shall stand forever"* (Dan. 2:44).

True world peace is possible only through the government of God and His shalom. The day is coming when the *"kingdoms of this world"* will *"become the kingdoms of our Lord and of His Christ, and He shall reign forever and ever"* (Rev. 11:15).

Isaiah's vision is that peace will be so prevalent that the land will be run by one named Shalom. Imagine electing "Shalom" as the president. But President Peace is not alone: Peace is flanked in the cabinet by Righteousness (or Justice) and Salvation (redemptive Liberation and Freedom) and Praise. We might rephrase: the kingdom's cabinet is governed by Peace, by Justice, by Freedom, and by God-directedness.[2]

I will make peace your governor and well-being your ruler. No longer will violence be heard in your land, nor ruin or destruction within your borders, but you will call your walls Salvation and your gates Praise (Isaiah 60:17-18 NIV).

The Garden of Eden was created on earth as a frontier outpost of heaven on earth.[3] The Living Word spoke shalom to the earth and order came through the work of the Holy Spirit. The Father willed, the Son spoke shalom, and the Holy Spirit performed what was spoken.

Eden was a dwelling place of God on earth where God communed with His children.[4] From the midst of Eden a river flowed out and split into four riverheads to water the Garden.[5] The living water first released in Genesis is still promised to us today.

In John 4:14, Jesus said to the woman at the well, *"Whoever drinks of the water that I shall give him will never thirst. But the water that I shall give him will become in him a fountain of water springing up into everlasting life."* However, Jesus merely said that the *mayim chayim*, living waters, gave everlasting life, *zoë*, but He did not explain what it was in this passage of Scripture until later in John 7.

In the temple during the Feast of Tabernacles, the feast celebrating God dwelling with His people, *"Jesus stood and said in a loud voice, 'Let anyone who is thirsty come to me and drink. Whoever believes in me, as Scripture has said, rivers of living water will flow from within them.' By this He meant the Spirit, whom those who believed in Him were later to receive. Up to that time the Spirit had not been given, since Jesus had not yet been glorified"* (John 7:37-39 NIV). This Scripture tells us here that the living water, therefore, is the Holy Spirit.

Jesus promised that the same river that flowed in Eden would spring up in believers and flow out from God enthroned within their hearts. When we turn from our sin and receive Jesus in our heart, we connect with the river of peace. The Lord begins the work of salvation within us. The Prince of Peace changes and rearranges us to bring order into the chaos of our life. Every area where Jesus establishes His lordship, His shalom replaces our disorder, fear, anger, disappointment, anxiety, lawlessness, and disharmony with God.

The river of shalom springs up as a fountain within us continually refreshing us with new life (see John 4:14). We can *stay connected* with supernatural peace that flows like a river. We can become *peacemakers* who share the good news of shalom with others. The ministry of the Spirit brings life and light and shalom, first to us, then to the world.

Information about this amazing peace is good to know, but how can it be a reality instead of theology? That is the reason this book was written. We want to make the river of peace as easily accessible to you as the natural water you drink. Finally, you can discover the secret to experiencing a lifestyle of supernatural, powerful peace, because *The Supernatural Power of Peace* gives you the how-tos you need!

ENDNOTES

1. W. Wilson, New Wilson's *Old Testament Word Studies* (Grand Rapids, MI: Kregel Publishers, 1987), 153.

2   S. McNight, "When Peace Like a River: Hope for Egypt," Christian Headlines, February 7, 2011. Accessed May 3, 2014 at http://www.christianheadlines.com/news/when-peace-like-a-river-hope-for-egypt-11645337.html.

3. The Garden of Eden, tabernacle of Moses, and the temple were types, or shadows, patterned after a heavenly reality. God showed Moses the heavenly tabernacle and cautioned him to build exactly like the pattern shown (see Exod. 25:8-9). Later, David gave his son Solomon the pattern for the temple (see 1 Chron. 28:10-12). They were designed by God—not man—to be copies of the sanctuary of God in heaven. T. Desmond Alexander, author of *From Eden to the New Jerusalem: An Introduction to Biblical Theology*, suggests that Genesis "portrays the Garden of Eden as a sanctuary or temple-garden" and as a "place where divinity and humanity enjoy each other's presence." Therefore, he continues, "It is appropriate that it should be a prototype for later Israelite sanctuaries. This explains why many of the decorative features of the tabernacle and temple are arboreal in nature." Even the menorah has a tree-like shape reminiscent of the Tree of Life. [T. D. Alexander, *From*

Eden to the New Jerusalem: An Introduction to Biblical Theology, (Grand Rapids, MI: Kregel Academic and Professional Publishing, 2009), 25.]

4.   The topography of the earth has been altered considerably since the time of the creation of the world. Natural disasters and floods have occurred. Tectonic plates have shifted. Rivers have dried up and the courses of other rivers have been changed. The Bible describes what could be tectonic/volcanic activity in the destruction of Sodom and Gomorrah in Abraham's day. Much time and effort has been expended in the attempt to find the location of the Garden of Eden. Looking to the Bible for clues, we find a great deal of support for Israel as the location of Eden. God clearly considers Israel to be His Holy land (see Ezek. 20:40). At the time of creation, Eden was His holy land. Abraham was told to sacrifice Isaac (a type of the sacrifice of Jesus) on Mount Moriah (see Gen. 22:2). Solomon built the temple "at Jerusalem at Mount Moriah" (see 2 Chron. 3:1). Jesus was crucified at Jerusalem. We can speculate that perhaps God sacrificed a lamb for a skin to cover Adam and Eve at the same location (see Gen. 3:21). If so, by extension, we can infer that the central point of the Garden of Eden was in the geographical region of Jerusalem. Many scholars have studied this topic extensively and there is much biblical support for this hypothesis in numerous books on the subject. [T. D. Alexander, *From Eden to the New Jerusalem: An Introduction to Biblical Theology*, (Grand Rapids, MI: Kregel Academic and Professional Publishing, 2009).]

5.   "In Jewish tradition, Israel was the center of the world, Jerusalem was the center of Israel, the temple was the center of Jerusalem, the Holy Place was the center of the temple, the Holy of Holies was the center of the Holy Place, and the foundation stone under the ark of the covenant was the center of the Holy of Holies. The creation of the world was said to have begun at the site of that stone, and it was believed that the prophesied living waters would spring from it." [C. S. Keener, *The Spirit in the Gospels and Acts: Divine Purity and Power,* (Peabody, MA: Hendrickson Publishers, 1997); see also D. Ward, "Rivers of Living Water," Grace and Knowledge: A Journal of Judeo-Christian History, Theology and Culture. Accessed on May 3, 2013, from http://graceandknowledge .faithweb.com/john7.html.]

PART I

WHO IS PEACE?

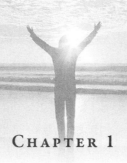

CHAPTER 1

PEACE IS A PERSON

By Dennis

A MAN WITHOUT A COUNTRY

Life as I had known it was over. I was like "a man without a country," ripped out of the long-term relationships in which I had become deeply entrenched and the familiar surroundings of small-town Pennsylvania. That's not to say there wasn't a mixture of profound pain I experienced along with the comfort of familiarity, but there is something deep within the human heart that yearns for a sufficient level of the status quo. Change is difficult for almost all of us. I felt disoriented. And yet I felt...peace.

I put the last suitcase in the trunk, slammed it shut, then turned around for one last look back. Taking a deep breath, I slid behind the wheel of my Dodge Neon, turned the key in the ignition, and left.

How had it come to this? On the surface perhaps, certainly to an outside observer, my life would have had the appearance of being picture perfect: a wife, two children, a nice house in a wonderful neighborhood, and many years serving as a pastor in a successful church I had planted and built from scratch. Few would have guessed that I had been struggling for years in a troubled marriage.

I had spent years praying, believing for a miracle, but no miracle ever happened. Now I had to choose my pain, for hard decisions always involve pain. There would be pain in staying and pain in going. But staying was no longer an option for me.

In the midst of all of this, I passionately loved God and had learned to truly rely upon Him. His presence was my daily balm and His peace my guide. Over the years, prior to making any decisions, I always presented my options to God from a position of neutrality. He taught me that my sense of peace would increase on the option He chose for my life.

Sometimes I would also feel a distinct check in my spirit, indicating a "no-go" from the Lord. Living in this manner, I had developed a track record of making right decisions, which gave me great confidence that God was ordering my steps according to His wisdom rather than my own intellect. This took place as I continually allowed the peace of God to rule in my heart (see Col. 3:15).

I had also learned how to let His healing waters flow to wash over my heart and calm any inner storms. So it wasn't that the pain was too great to go on, I just couldn't do it anymore. Living a lie no longer worked. I wasn't able to pull it off any longer. Some would say "the grace had lifted."

In the spring of 1997, my 25-year marriage came to an end and I resigned from the pastorate. Although I had worked numerous jobs before I was a pastor, serving the Lord was all I really knew or ever wanted to do. What now? I was sure of one thing only, that God would never leave or forsake me (see Heb. 13:5). Now it was up to God to act on my behalf.

Over the years I had made knowing God—really knowing Him—the number-one priority of my life. I didn't just learn *about* Him, I focused on learning all the nuances of His presence and becoming aware of the whispers of the Holy Spirit. In my morning prayer times, I was attentive to every subtle variance of His presence He revealed to me, but *always* felt a sense of His peace both in prayer and in daily life.

Early in my Christian life the Lord had admonished me, "Don't let anything come between what you and I have together." Therefore, I took great care to deal quickly with anything that temporarily interrupted the sense of supernatural peace I experienced when I was in His presence. *"He Himself is our peace,"* Paul said (Eph. 2:14). Therefore experiencing peace is an assurance of His nearness. Peace is a Person, and when I was with Him I felt His peace.

The Lord trained me to be sensitive to His voice and the awareness of His presence. He would awaken me in the middle of the night with the featherlight brush of His presence. Although I am a heavy sleeper, I hold prompt obedience to the Lord as one of my most cherished values. With my weary body still heavy with sleep, I would slide my leg off the bed, letting gravity do its work until I was kneeling by the side of the bed to meet with Him in prayer.

One day during this difficult time, as was my habitual practice, I went for a walk in a local park. My thoughts were somber on that dreary, overcast March day, which was so typical of western Pennsylvania weather. The Lord suddenly startled me by quickening a comforting assurance that, regardless of how much He hated divorce (see Mal. 2:16), He would still walk with me no matter what. My eyes brimmed with tears as my heart was warmed by His reassurance.

Work? I felt like a failure and wondered what I would do. I wondered how my calling to ministry and service to God could be reconciled with my present circumstances. Could people ever accept a divorced pastor? With no church or ministry, how would I make a living? When I first began ministry God had told me He would always meet all my financial needs, saying, "You will never see secular employment again." But I couldn't help but wonder if that still applied to my life. I knew the Bible was full of conditional promises—"If you do this...I will do that for you"—but was this one of those conditional promises? I had many questions but few answers.

With only a few months' worth of savings in my bank account, it was difficult to comprehend how the Lord could ever fulfill this promise. Yet, inexplicably, I had hope in my heart that God could still bring beauty out of ashes and joy out of mourning (see Isa. 61:3).

One thing I didn't understand, however, were words spoken to me through a prophet visiting a local church in January of that year. He had singled me out of a crowd and prophesied that the coming year would be a year of jubilee for me and that God would bring restoration into my life. That seemed outrageously impossible and confusing, yet I knew the anointing was on his words.

The Lord also encouraged me through Micah 7:8-9, saying, *"When I fall, I will arise; when I sit in darkness, the Lord will be a light to me. ...He will bring me forth to the light; I will see His righteousness."* This was easier for me to understand than the concept of a personal jubilee. In spite of my situation, God was telling me to get up and allow Him to reveal each step I should take. Even in my darkness, God would be my light.

I was aware that my life was in chaos, but I also knew I had heard from God. It was just difficult to imagine how God could "fix" my broken life. As I wondered how long the promised restoration might take—five, ten, or fifteen years—God amazed me by interrupting my train of thought to say He had other plans and would restore me within *one* year. I didn't even know what to think because the very idea seemed incomprehensible to me.

JUST LIKE ABRAHAM

For years I'd been drawn to the description of Abraham in Hebrews 11:8: *"By faith Abraham obeyed when he was called to go out to the place which he would receive as an inheritance. And he went out, not knowing where he was headed."* Abraham paid a big price to obey God and receive his promised inheritance.

It was unsettling enough that Abraham was called to fulfill a destiny he didn't understand and had to wait until hope had all but died for a promised son. However, he also had to leave behind family and all that was comfortable and familiar and set out for an unknown destination (see Gen. 12:1-2). The Lord did say he would end up in *"a land that I will show you,"* but it would have been nice to have a few more details before he departed on his journey. Of course, we now know that the story had a happy ending. God fulfilled His promise: *"I will bless you and make your name great; and you shall be a blessing"* (Gen. 12:2).

Like Abraham before me, I was sensing God leading me to leave what had been my comfort zone in Pennsylvania and venture out to a new territory, both geographically and spiritually. However, it was hard to be confident my story would have a happy ending like Abraham's. I hoped God would somehow bless me and make me a blessing again to others, but, to tell you the truth, I couldn't imagine how things could possibly turn out so well for me because of my circumstances.

Relocation seemed like my only option. Of that I had no doubt. But where would I go? Without a single idea why, I felt a deepening desire to move to Charlotte, North Carolina. Every time I thought about Charlotte, I sensed an increase in the presence and peace of God. The Lord didn't give me any details, but He quickened Jeremiah 29:7 to my heart. He impressed upon me both an assignment and a promise: *"Seek the peace of the city where I have caused you to be carried away captive, and pray to the Lord for it; for in its peace you will have peace."*

Charlotte was a totally unfamiliar city to me. I had never visited it before, nor did I know a single soul who lived there. I had never even been to the South before. Much as I would have liked a ready-made support system at this point in my life, God was leaving me no other option but to trust in Him alone. I knew no one in Charlotte and I had no plans for what I was to do when I arrived there. No family. No friends. No job. No ministry. Charlotte was no more than a point on the map to me. Nevertheless, in March of 1997 I packed up some belongings in my car and departed for a future full of nothing but question marks, to a location hundreds of miles away from my roots.

When I left Pennsylvania that day, life had an eerie quality about it, almost as though I were living in a dream. I felt rootless and aimless. For more than 30 years I had lived in the same town, drove the same route to work every day, went to the same gas station, got my hair cut at the same place, and used the same bank. I networked with a great group of local pastors, some of whom had become close friends. I was living life almost on autopilot.

While I was very disquieted with the uncertainty of the position in which I now found myself, I was also aware of a solemn responsibility to follow the leading of the Lord. I desired to obey God no matter what He asked of me. My entire life belonged fully to Him. There is also a price to pay for saying no to God. (Consider the unfortunate outcomes experienced by Esau and Jonah because of their disobedience.)

I was also aware that comfort zones can become coffins if we aren't willing to let go of our own ideas to follow the call of God. I had the uncomfortable sensation of being in a position like the four lepers who asked themselves: *"Why do we sit here until we die?"* (2 Kings 7:3 NASB). Staying would mean eventual "death" while leaving in obedience to God would mean a new life.

But why Charlotte? Why had God impressed *this* city upon my heart? When friends asked for my new contact information, I couldn't even give them an address or phone number. (Cell phones were not as commonplace then as they are now.) I am sure some of them thought I was deluded. As I approached the city God had said was a place for a new beginning, I felt very alone.

However, something extraordinary happened when I crossed the state line into North Carolina. In a flash, in my mind's eye, I saw a city map of Charlotte suddenly burst into flames, just like the Ponderosa map in the opening sequence of the popular *Bonanza* television series many years ago. God gives big confirmation for big decisions. I didn't know exactly what the map in flames meant, but I knew it was good and that God must have something significant in store for me. Though this was a great encouragement that the Lord had something special in mind for me in Charlotte, I still couldn't escape the nagging thought that I had absolutely no idea what the future might hold.

LEAD ME, LORD

I do not have a good sense of direction, and that's an understatement. Fortunately, I can read a map, but getting around in any new city is a major trial for me. Not knowing my way around Charlotte, I drove straight through the city on I-77. When I suddenly noticed the sign for Exit 1, I realized I needed to get off the freeway immediately or else I'd drive right past Charlotte into South Carolina and have to backtrack.

"Lead me, Lord!" I whispered in a quick prayer. Without any particular destination in mind, I turned onto the exit ramp and continued to drive. I knew of several churches in the area and wanted to find my church home before proceeding with other decisions that would affect my future there. I believe in having my priorities in proper order: God first, my personal needs second.

Somehow, I ended up on South Polk Street on the southern edge of the city. To this day, I can't imagine how I ended up there. When I noticed a small metal building with children's playground equipment and cars parked outside, I felt impressed to stop and ask for directions to a local church with which I was familiar.

As I turned into the parking lot, I noticed a man sitting in one of the cars. I pulled up beside him and rolled down the car window, but before I could even get a word out, the man rolled down his own window and said, "Are you going to ask for directions? The Lord told me to wait in the car and not go in, because someone was going to ask me for directions, and I needed to be here." Before I pulled away, he explained that he was there to attend a prayer meeting in the little building.

The man's statement surprised and encouraged me. My heart was flooded with peace and gratitude that God was giving me so many hopeful signs. Immediately my feeling of being cut adrift left, and I was filled with the certainty that God was still very much with me. Although I still felt the strangeness of my situation, I had complete confidence that my heavenly Father was in complete control of my life. Despite the fact that I was still in the dark about what steps to take, I was becoming more and more sure that the Lord had a good future planned for me. With every twist and turn of my journey, He was directing my path.

Little did I know that I would soon meet Jen, we would get married, and together we would embark on the most wonderful phase of our life. (Later, Jen walked around for a full year just shaking her head and saying, "I am *so* impressed with God!")

GUIDED BY HIS PEACE

The truth is that, even though I felt so many things during this season of my life, God was guiding me with His supernatural peace. Throughout the years, I've learned to trust in His peace continually, allowing it to affect every decision I make and guide me in every circumstance of life. God's peace isn't something we're to rely on intermittently to alleviate anxious thoughts or get us through troubling situations. The lifestyle of walking in God's peace should be a 24/7 experience for us.

I want to encourage you that it is possible to experience this supernatural lifestyle of peace through every moment of every day. I'm not saying that you won't have times when you temporarily lose your peace, but when those times come it is extremely easy to get right back into it. The truth is that God's peace governs us, guides us, guards us, gathers people around us, and grounds us in all that we do. I've now walked in this supernatural lifestyle of peace for more than 35 years, learning how to commune with God in intimacy and experiencing His supernatural peace throughout my days.

Peace is not a mysterious attribute of God that is only experienced occasionally. It is an attribute of God, to be sure, but it is a practical and tangible attribute that we can experience in our daily lives. Peace isn't simply the absence of conflict or hostility. We often say we're peaceful if the children are at school or we're on a vacation at the beach. But it is my belief that we can experience God's peace even in the midst of chaos.

Experiencing God's peace doesn't require a tranquil environment. His peace can be experienced in a war zone, a factory, an office, or at home. God's supernatural peace can be tangibly experienced in church as well as while driving in the car or working a job in the marketplace. God's peace transcends all of our circumstances, carnal emotions, and geographical locations. It is my desire to demystify the peace of God and how it relates to our lives.

LEARNING FROM BROTHER LAWRENCE

Brother Lawrence (1614 to 1691) was a monk in a Carmelite monastery in Paris. After he died, his letters were compiled into a book called *The Practice of the Presence of God*. It became one of the most popular Christian books of all time, among both Catholics and Protestants alike. This humble man, who lived hundreds of years ago, has become a tremendous example for me, mentoring me in supernatural peace.

Brother Lawrence sought to spend his entire life in unceasing adoration and communion with God in every thought he had, word he spoke, and action he performed. Loving God became the central theme and purpose of his life. Even while engaging in the mundane chores and activities of life, like washing dishes or cooking an omelet, Brother Lawrence sought to glorify God and experience His supernatural presence in a tangible way.

His Christlike example caused Brother Lawrence to stand out among his peers. He gained a reputation for living in such intimacy with God that he constantly experienced profound peace. For him, prayer wasn't just something to cross off a to-do list each morning, but rather Someone he communed with and deeply loved. He truly lived in a lifestyle of communion with God, meaning he lived a lifestyle of supernatural peace.

If we are going to live lives saturated with the peace of God, then we must understand the true nature of peace. Peace is a Person with whom we can commune on a continual basis. Paul said, *"He Himself is our peace"* (Eph. 2:14). In order to experience this lifestyle of peace I'm writing about, we must have an ongoing intimate relationship with the Father.

PEACE IS A PERSON

Many of us don't understand what the peace of God really is. We think it is the absence of conflict, where everything seems to be going well for us, and we don't have too many things to worry about at the moment. And because everything seems to be going fine, we feel pretty peaceful at the moment. But once we experience a test or a trial, we "lose" our peace and wonder what we're going to do.

But peace isn't just an emotion we experience in order to bring relaxation to our bodies or souls, like we're on an emotional vacation, for little moments throughout the day. It's not only something we long to sense when our car breaks down or when the house needs to be cleaned. We should not only want to return to the peace of God when it is absent, but it should be something that pervades our souls. And peace is extremely practical for how we live our day-to-day lives.

Many of us know that Paul said, *"Be anxious for nothing, but in everything by prayer and supplication, with thanksgiving, let your requests be made known to God; and the peace of God, which surpasses all understanding, will guard your hearts and minds through Christ Jesus"* (Phil. 4:6-7). So we understand that peace is to guard our hearts, and we know that it somehow surpasses our understanding. But how does it do this?

There is a close connection between prayer and experiencing God's peace. Paul says that we're to turn all of our anxious thoughts into prayer, and as we commune with the Lord of heaven and earth a supernatural peace will enter our hearts and guard our minds. Brother Lawrence sought to live a life in continual communion with God, which enabled him to live in a lifestyle of supernatural peace. This is why, even in the midst of his mundane chores, he could experience the depths of God through communion with Him.

Likewise, in order for us to experience the lifestyle of 24/7 peace, we must understand what peace is and where it comes from. Again, peace is a Person. Peace comes because Jesus is the *"Prince of Peace"* (Isa. 9:6). And it is only by communing with the Prince of Peace on a daily basis that we learn to live and walk in this peace, receiving Him in our hearts.

If we think that peace can only come when there is an absence of conflict, when everything seems to be going right, then we'll rarely experience the peace of God. In fact, it will be an emotion that always seems to evade us because things will not always align outwardly.

If peace is based upon the tranquil surroundings, then my experience of God's peace will be very minimal indeed. But if I understand that God's peace comes because Jesus is the Prince of Peace, I can experience it much more often and in a deeper way. If it is not based on my outward circumstances and in fact changes my *response* to my outward circumstances, then I'm able to experience peace at any point during the day.

If peace comes by communing with God, then we can do that continuously. Paul admonishes us to *"pray without ceasing"* (1 Thess. 5:17). Our mind cannot think about God all the time, but our spirit has the ability to continually commune with Him. Peace is a Person with whom we walk in an ongoing relationship.

PEACE SWALLOWS CIRCUMSTANCES

Because I'm in a personal relationship with the Prince of Peace, I can now experience Him—meaning I can now experience peace—no matter my outward circumstances. For example, the day before Jen and I were supposed to leave for an extended ministry trip to Connecticut in October of 2008, Jen turned on the computer at 5:00 in the morning to do some administrative tasks before we left. Or at least she tried to. Nothing happened. Then I came over and tried to turn it on too, only to experience the same result—a black screen.

We didn't have time to take it to the shop, and our secretary would need to use it for ministry business while we were gone. Jen stayed in peace, however, by releasing the situation into the hands of God, communing with Him and trusting Him in the midst of what otherwise should have been an anxious situation.

It was too early to do anything, so she felt led to look through the yellow pages in the phone book. One computer repair ad stood out more than the others—it said to call after 8:00 a.m.

The ad also mentioned that they would do on-site repairs. As soon as the clock struck 8:00, Jen called.

The owner said he was only there between 8:00 and 8:30 that morning, then he would be out the rest of the day. He said that Jen had called at the perfect time before his day was completely booked. Jen explained our situation to him, our time frame, and how our secretary needed to use the computer while we were gone. He said he was a Christian and would come by at noon. He was there promptly and repaired our computer within 30 minutes.

On that same trip, we checked in at the hotel in Manchester, Connecticut. After we unpacked, we returned to our car only to discover that our window was smashed and our GPS was missing. It seems that thieves swept through the area, targeting hotel parking lots. We called the number on the insurance card only to be informed that it would take at least a week to get that particular window in stock.

A week without a car window? What about the infamous New England weather that could change at any moment? We released it into the hands of God and chose to stay in peace. I suddenly felt prompted to call our local agent in Fort Mill, South Carolina. He made some calls and had a window for us the next day. Then someone bought a new GPS as a gift for us. Even though there were some circumstances that could have easily caused us to lose our peace, we decided to trust in the Lord, allowing His peace to guard our hearts.

No matter what circumstances we may face in our lives, we can experience the supernatural peace of God in a tangible and real way. Peace is not dependent on our circumstances, but upon the Person and work of Jesus Christ. If we will remain in communion with Him, then the Prince of Peace will invade our hearts, enabling us to walk in a lifestyle of supernatural peace every moment of every day.

THE KINGDOM OF PEACE

By Dr. Jen

JESUS ESTABLISHES A KINGDOM OF PEACE

When Jesus rules, peace is the result because He *is* Peace (see Eph. 2:14). Wherever He extends the scepter of His authority, radical spiritual, societal, and cosmic peace follow. If we see discord and disorder, His kingdom has not yet fully come in that area. When peace impacts our world, the nations turn to God. When peace impacts us personally, we experience wholeness within and harmony without.

Can you imagine what it would be like for Jesus to rule the world? The Bible tells of such a day:

Now it shall come to pass in the latter days that the mountain of the Lord's house shall be established on

the top of the mountains, and shall be exalted above the
hills; and all nations shall flow to it. Many people shall
come and say, "Come, and let us go up to the mountain
of the Lord, to the house of the God of Jacob; He will
teach us His ways, and we shall walk in His paths."
For out of Zion shall go forth the law, and the word of
the Lord from Jerusalem. He shall judge between the
nations, and rebuke many people; they shall beat their
swords into plowshares, and their spears into pruning
hooks; nation shall not lift up sword against nation,
neither shall they learn war anymore (Isaiah 2:2-4).

Someday, as Isaiah prophesied, this invisible kingdom will come to earth in its fullness, *"for out of Zion shall go forth the law."*

If Jesus ruled the world and judged righteously among the nations, how would He govern? All law is based on a philosophy, or worldview, and built on a foundation. If God built a nation, what would be the supreme law of the land? The Bible, of course. Within it we find the basis of spiritual, religious, and civil government.

The Declaration of Independence refers to "the laws of Nature and Nature's God," or what is called *natural law*. Natural law is a "rule of conduct arising out of the natural relations of human beings, established by the Creator.... The foundation of this law is...the will of God, discovered by right reason, and aided by divine revelation; and its principles...apply with equal obligation to individuals and to nations.... [It is] a rule which so necessarily agrees with the nature and state of man that, without observing its maxims, the peace and happiness of society can never be preserved."[1]

Therefore, the eternal principles of the Creator of the universe are embedded into the universe itself. When these principles are retrieved from the realm of the eternal and encoded in civil law, the result is government according to natural law, or government under God.

Cicero (106-143 BC) was a Roman philosopher, orator, and statesman who had the revelation that man had been given the capacity to reach up into the lofty realm of the cosmos, learn the principles of right government, and apply them in just law for civil society. Thomas Jefferson later echoed the terminology of Cicero when he wrote The Declaration of Independence. Human nature included the capacity for logical reasoning, which could in turn discover justice, and this formed the basis for law. Cicero defined natural law as "true law." True law is perceived by rational thought that receives and applies the eternal and fixed law of God that governs the universe.

Cicero called these truths "self-evident." Jefferson wrote, "We hold these truths to be self-evident." Even though he lived in a pagan culture that worshiped many gods, he had a revelation of the attributes of the one true God, His love and goodness, and man's duty to love and obey God and serve his fellow man. How could Cicero have learned without a teacher? The Bible tells us that God has written truth in creation itself, which can be read by those who seek to know:

> *For that which is known about God is evident to them and made plain in their inner consciousness, because God [Himself] has shown it to them. For ever since the creation of the world His invisible nature and*

attributes, that is, His eternal power and divinity,
have been made intelligible and clearly discernible
in and through the things that have been made (His
handiworks). So [men] are without excuse [altogether
without any defense or justification] (Romans 1:19-20
AMP).

What is this peace that rules nations? It is nothing other
than the shalom of God. When Jesus rules and reigns, His kingdom is established—and shalom is present. The Hebrew word
for peace, *shalom,* is so much richer than our English definition; it means wholeness, everything is intact, and nothing is
out of order. It includes completeness, divine health, peace,
welfare, safety, soundness, tranquility, prosperity, increase,
perfectness, fullness, rest, harmony, the absence of agitation
or discord, no injustice, and no pain. No wonder shalom is
used as the traditional Jewish greeting and farewell. Speaking
shalom over a person's life blesses them with all the goodness
that comes from God.

The kingdom of God and the shalom of God are synonymous, for where Jesus is Lord His shalom is present as well. Chaos
cannot resist the power of shalom. Shalom swallows up evil and
chaos and establishes the rule of Christ. When the kingdom
comes, shalom comes. When shalom comes, the kingdom comes.

Jesus said to His disciples, *"But seek first the kingdom of God*
and His righteousness, and all these things shall be added to you"
(Matt. 6:33). When Jesus told us to seek the kingdom of God,
He meant that by seeking the kingdom we would, as a byprod-
uct, receive everything the kingdom contains. So seeking the

kingdom of God is equivalent to seeking the shalom of God, for where His kingdom is, everything is intact and harmonious; there is nothing missing or lacking.

Most people today think about peace in terms of pleasant surroundings. Peace happens when things are going smoothly, they don't have to do major repairs on their house or car, their bank account has an adequate amount of money in it, and the children are all doing fairly well.

However, when Jesus rules our life, we can enjoy supernatural peace regardless of difficult circumstances and unpleasant people. When we possess supernatural peace, we have the assurance that Jesus is ruling in our hearts and minds, empowering us to live under the lordship of Jesus Christ moment by moment. And when we yield to God and trust Him to be in charge of our life, we possess supernatural peace. It is impossible to trust God and be stressed at the same time.

VISION FOR THE COMING DAYS

What would it mean for us if the kingdom of God were truly established in our personal life? Our inner life would be ruled by shalom. With Jesus in control, we would have no agendas and use no manipulation. Our trust in God would be absolute and we could find our rest in Him. Our inner reality affects the world around us, spreading outward like the ripples on a pond.

In the coming days, entering the rest of God will become more vital than ever before. God is shaking everything that can be shaken so that only His unshakeable kingdom will remain.

He has promised, saying, "Yet once more I shake not only the earth, but also heaven." Now this, "Yet once more," indicates the removal of those things that are being shaken, as of things that are made, that the things which cannot be shaken may remain. Therefore, since we are receiving a kingdom which cannot be shaken, let us have grace, by which we may serve God acceptably with reverence and godly fear. For our God is a consuming fire (Hebrews 12:26-29).

When our top priority becomes the kingdom of God and His righteousness, then all of the blessings of shalom will be added to us. The full embodiment of everything that's *kingdom* will be imparted to us.

What could happen if a company of bold peacemakers arose with hearts that burned with zeal for the coming of the kingdom of God on earth? Jesus's heart would become our heart. His mission would become our mission. We would be able to envision shalom coming to the world around us and see into the future of shalom that will be established in the last days. We could become co-laborers with the Lord to bring His kingdom to the nations.

Let's further define what we mean when we say the kingdom of God is synonymous with the peace of God.

SAR SHALOM

Isaiah prophesied about the coming of Jesus Christ in human flesh over 600 years before He was placed in a manger in Bethlehem. In this passage of Scripture, Jesus is described as the Prince of Peace—Sar Shalom—whose government and peace will always increase. Isaiah said:

> *For to us a Child is born, to us a Son is given; and the government shall be upon His shoulder, and His name shall be called Wonderful Counselor, Mighty God, Everlasting Father [of Eternity], Prince of Peace [Sar Shalom]. Of the increase of His government and of peace there shall be no end, upon the throne of David and over his kingdom, to establish it and to uphold it with justice and with righteousness from the [latter] time forth, even forevermore. The zeal of the Lord of hosts will perform this* (Isaiah 9:6-7 AMP).

Jesus was born as the *Son of Man* in earthly humanity. He was begotten as the *Son of God* in heavenly deity, the God of glory. His government is powerful, eternal, and complete. He cannot be voted in or voted out, for He is Sovereign Lord. His name is *Wonderful*, "wonderful, miracle working, awe-inspiring, God who does marvels." He is the great *Counselor*, who plans and executes the eternal purposes of God.

As *Mighty God*, He is the valiant man of war and great military hero (see Isa. 42:13) who goes forth into battle as the King of kings and Lord of lords (see Rev. 19:15-16). He is the *Eternal Father* of a new race of men. As *Prince of Peace*, Sar Shalom, He is the Lord who brought peace out of chaos and the One still commanding, "Peace, be still."

The very Lord and embodiment of peace will stretch forth and expand a kingdom of peace that will have no end. The zeal of the *Lord of Hosts*, Jehovah-Sabaoth, will accomplish this together with His army of angels and a great company of peacemakers.

When Jesus came upon the earth, although He was the Suffering Servant spoken of in Isaiah 53, He was also a King who came to establish a heavenly kingdom on earth. Isaiah proclaims that He is the Prince of Peace, the One who still commands peace to come in the midst of chaos, the One who is still in charge of peace. And because Jesus came as a Prince, He must be a Prince over *something*. And that something is a kingdom, a realm where He reigns supreme.

When we understand the authority of Jesus as the Prince of Peace, His words take on a much more profound meaning: *"Peace I leave with you, My peace I give to you; not as the world gives do I give to you. Let not your heart be troubled, neither let it be afraid"* (John 14:27). Jesus's peace is not a product of this world—He brought it from another realm, that of heaven.

The kingdom of God is the triumphant manifestation of supernatural peace that will someday embrace all creation. Jesus was the living expression of the kingdom on earth through His life and ministry. He instructed His disciples to pray for His kingdom to come and His will to be done *"on earth as it is in heaven"* (Matt. 6:10), and He sent them forth to continue His work of kingdom building. The Holy Spirit empowers us with supernatural peace to be worthy ambassadors of shalom for the increase of the kingdom of God.

CREATING SHALOM
OUT OF CHAOS

The scene God surveyed from the vantage point of heaven was formless and empty—a newly created earth covered with tumultuous waters and pitch-black darkness. The earth was *"without form, and void; and darkness was on the face of the deep"* (Gen. 1:2). Nothing could inhabit this unorganized mass of swirling water and disorder.

When the Bible says that the earth was *"formless and void,"* the Hebrew phrase, *tohu wa-bohu,* conveys the concept of something that is desolate, chaotic, empty, void, undistinguishable, without purpose, without order, without meaning, a total ruin, and in utter and complete anarchy. There is no English word that completely captures this idea, though "chaos" is used in most of our English translations. The word "chaos," *ra* in Hebrew, is the opposite of shalom. It can be translated as bad, evil, wicked, or complete chaos. With *ra*, everything is wrong. When there is shalom, however, everything is right.

The Spirit of God hovered over the waters, waiting with anticipation. Suddenly, a sound like mighty rushing waters roared throughout the universe. Out of the communion within the Godhead, Sar Shalom spoke, "Peace!" The One who governs and commands shalom worked His mastery and transformation began.

When Jesus spoke His powerful word into the atmosphere and to the chaotic particles of the universe, shalom took the ascendancy—alignment began, order was created, elements came together, and the earth took shape. The Prince of Peace spoke into the *ra*, the chaos, and suddenly shalom dominated. Alignment came. Order came. The chaos was stopped and replaced by harmony between all things.

The writer of Hebrews says that Jesus is *"the brightness of* [the Father's] *glory and the express image of His person."* He upholds *"all things by the word of His power"* (Heb. 1:3). The Amplified Bible sheds more light on this passage of Scripture:

> *[But] in the last of these days He has spoken to us in [the person of a] Son, Whom He appointed Heir and lawful Owner of all things, also by and through Whom He created the worlds and the reaches of space and the ages of time [He made, produced, built, operated, and arranged them in order]. [Jesus] is the sole expression of the glory of God [the Light-being, the out-raying or radiance of the divine], and He is the perfect imprint and very image of [God's] nature, upholding and maintaining and guiding and propelling the universe by His mighty word of power* (Hebrews 1:2-3 AMP).

The Lord Jesus Christ, *"Heir and lawful owner of all things,"* who *"created the worlds and the reaches of space and the ages of time"* is *"upholding, maintaining, guiding, and propelling the universe by His mighty word of power."* If He ever stopped speaking shalom, all the elements of the universe would explode back into chaos. He holds together and sustains all things (present tense—even right now) with His word of shalom.

Not only did He do this at the time of creation, but the entire created order still testifies to His work. This is why the psalmist wrote:

The heavens declare the glory of God; the skies proclaim the work of His hands. Day after day they pour forth speech; night after night they reveal knowledge (Psalms 19:1-3 NIV).

The Bible gives the account of an evening when Jesus got into a boat with His disciples and told them to cross over to the other side of the lake. They launched out, and as they sailed Jesus fell asleep because He was tired after ministering to the multitudes. Suddenly a great windstorm arose, and the boat began to fill with water. The disciples were afraid the boat would sink—and Jesus just slept in the midst of it all. They awoke Him, saying, "Master, Master, we are perishing!"

Jesus didn't suddenly wake up, panic, and tell all the guys to grab buckets so they could bail the water out of the boat. Jesus simply arose, rebuked the waves and the wind, *"and they ceased, and there was calm.... And* [the disciples] *were afraid, and marveled, saying to one another, 'Who can this be? For He commands even the winds and water, and they obey Him!'"* (Luke 8:24-25).

Notice that Jesus rebuked the storm. Is it possible that catastrophic weather comes from the demonic realm? Prior to the fall, weather was ruled by shalom in the Garden of Eden where everything was good and perfect. The Living Word of God, Jesus Christ, spoke to His creation and it obeyed Him. Jesus is the Prince of Peace and therefore brings order out of chaos, establishing shalom within the created order. Jesus reigns in the midst of His kingdom to bring shalom in the midst of *ra*. The disciples were well acquainted with the story of creation and knew of the One who had authority to calm wind and wave. *"Who can this be?"* Only the Prince of Peace.

WHAT IS THE KINGDOM?

What makes heaven *heaven*? Heaven is a realm filled with the love and glory of God, where God's will is perfectly obeyed. God's will is not just His commandments, ideas, or plans. The will of God is a flow of His divine purposes. The kingdom is the very nature of heaven brought to earth. Jesus came to do His Father's will and bring the kingdom of God to earth. As Christians, we are called to do the same. Andrew Murray defines God's will this way:

> In the will of God, we have the perfect expression of His divine perfection. Because He is the fountain of all beauty and blessedness, His will is inconceivably beautiful and blessed. His divine wisdom and goodness are made known through it. Through it alone can man know his God. In accepting and doing God's will, man finds the only and the sure way to fellowship and union with the Father.
>
> The glory and the blessedness of heaven consist of nothing but this—God's will is done therein and by all. There is nothing to hinder God's working His blessed will in countless hosts. Those to whom He wills goodness, blessedness, and service, surrender their whole being in submission and adoration. God lives in them and they in God. They are filled with the fullness of God. In the Lord's Prayer, our Blessed

Master teaches us to come to the Father with the wonderful petition that His will may be done on earth, even "as it is in heaven"![2]

George Whitefield (1714-1770) was an English Anglican evangelist and powerful orator who spread the fire of the First Great Awakening across Great Britain and the American colonies. Whitefield preached that the doctrines of Christ are, in their essence, doctrines of peace:

> The doctrines of the gospel are doctrines of peace, and they bring comfort to all who believe in them.... The spirit of the world is hatred; that of Christ is love; the spirit of the world is vexation; that of Christ is pleasure: the spirit of the world is sorrow; that of Christ is joy: the spirit of the world is evil, and that of Christ is good: the spirit of the world will never satisfy us, but Christ's Spirit is all satisfaction: the spirit of the world is misery; that of Christ is ease.[3]

Shalom happens when the teachings of Christ are put into practice. In other words, if we abide in Christ and obey His teachings, shalom is the result—all things come into order and our relationships with God and man become harmonious. We can even be instruments of God's peace for our enemies if we obey the Scriptures. The Son of God loved and forgave as He was nailed to a cross. He says to us, *"I say to you, love your enemies, bless those who curse you, do good to those who hate you, and pray for those who spitefully use you and persecute you, that you may be sons of your Father in heaven"* (Matt. 5:44-45).

When the disciples asked Jesus to teach them to pray, He said, *"In this manner, therefore, pray: Our Father in heaven, hallowed be Your name. Your kingdom come. Your will be done on earth as it is in heaven"* (Matt. 6:9-10). He taught them to pray for the kingdom of God to come, releasing shalom into every circumstance of life.

The kingdom of God exists in any place or person where God's rule is obeyed and accepted as supreme. It is important to note that the church has been given a significant role in advancing God's kingdom on the earth. God's kingdom and rule are exercised through the church. The church is a subset of the kingdom, but it is not the kingdom itself.

We help advance the kingdom of God in the earth through our prayers and through what we do as emissaries of the Lord. *"Of the increase of His government and peace there will be no end"* (Isa. 9:7). We have the responsibility to surrender to the rule of God in our own lives and co-labor with the Lord to establish peace on earth.

THE KINGDOM: GOD'S PLAN TO RESTORE SHALOM TO THE WORLD

The kingdom of God was perfectly expressed in the Garden of Eden before the fall of man. Sin shattered the harmony of shalom, but God had a plan to restore shalom to the world. The kingdom of God is not a unique concept to the New Testament. The Bible says that the kingdom of God was established since before the foundation of the world (see Matt. 25:33-34). Isaiah spoke of this kingdom over 600 years before the birth of Jesus as the Son of Man. The kingdom is a spiritual kingdom that will only increase. Jesus said, *"My kingdom is not of this world"* (John 18:36).

Jesus was sent for this very purpose—to establish His kingdom of peace in the hearts and lives of men and women all around the world. He came to preach the good news of the kingdom of God: *"I must preach the kingdom of God...for this purpose I have been sent"* (Luke 4:43).

From the very beginning of Jesus's ministry, He preached the good news of the kingdom of God. After John baptized Him in the Jordan, Jesus began to preach and say, *"Repent, for the kingdom of heaven is at hand"* (Matt. 4:17). What kingdom was He talking about? A kingdom that originated in heaven and that was full of shalom.

Not only did Jesus's words proclaim the kingdom of God, but every miracle He performed demonstrated the coming of the kingdom as well as the presence of heaven invading the earth in Spirit and power. During the time of Jesus's ministry on earth, He brought order and healing to those who suffered from sickness and disease and deliverance to those tormented by demons: *"But if I cast out demons with the finger of God, surely the kingdom has come upon you"* (Luke 11:20).

Matthew sums up Jesus's ministry (note the connection between preaching and the demonstration of power in the below verses):

> *And Jesus went about all Galilee, teaching in their synagogues, preaching the gospel of the kingdom, and*

healing all kinds of sickness and all kinds of disease among the people (Matthew 4:23).

Then Jesus went about all the cities and villages, teaching in their synagogues, preaching the gospel of the kingdom, and healing every sickness and every disease among the people (Matthew 9:35).

Next, Jesus sent His disciples forth to preach the kingdom of God, heal those who were sick, cast out demons, and to raise the dead (see Matt. 10:8). Just as Jesus was sent to the earth to reveal the kingdom of God through His words and deeds, so Jesus sent His disciples to do the same: *"He sent them to preach the kingdom of God and to heal the sick"* (Luke 9:2). They were to demonstrate the very kingdom Jesus came to initiate, namely, a kingdom of shalom—to speak to the chaos in the world, thus restoring order.

After Jesus's resurrection, He continued to teach His disciples about *"the things concerning the kingdom of God"* (Acts 1:3 NASB). Luke wrote the Book of Acts to give an account of *"all that Jesus began both to do and teach, until the day in which He was taken up, after He through the Holy Spirit had given commandments to the apostles whom He had chosen, to whom He also presented Himself alive after His suffering by many infallible proofs, being seen by them during forty days and speaking of the things pertaining to the kingdom of God"* (Acts 1:1-3).

The priority of Jesus after the cross was the same as before it—preach the good news of the kingdom and demonstrate that kingdom by the works He did.

SEEK FIRST HIS KINGDOM

It is God's desire that we become partners with Him in His mission—to help establish the kingdom of peace upon the earth. When we make it our number one priority to be about our heavenly Father's business, we too will *"seek first the kingdom of God and His righteousness"* (Matt. 6:33). Those who are obedient to the will of God will lack no good thing.

Each of us are called to be an extension of the kingdom of God in this earth, releasing peace into a troubled world. The first step we must take is to make shalom a lifestyle. Every small step of obedience builds spiritual prowess. We can live as peacemakers who change the world for the better. This is truly possible.

Annika was with some relatives in the hospital in Northbridge, Massachusetts in 2004, and one of them had an angry meltdown and was completely out of control. Having been to many of our classes and meetings where we taught about the power of peace, she decided, "I am going to change this bad atmosphere in here." Annika did not just stay in peace, she became militant in order to create peace. First, she dropped down to Jesus in her heart, and then released rivers of peace and love. Peace flooded the room, and the angry woman's behavior changed radically and became perfectly calm. Annika understood that Jesus establishes a kingdom of peace.

After attending some of our classes in Connecticut, a pastor told us that he was in line to make a purchase at a convenience store, standing about four people back from the cashier. The clerk was particularly rude and surly to each customer. The pastor thought, "I am going to try what I heard Dennis and Jen say in the class." So the pastor let a river of peace and love flow toward the clerk, and by the time it was the pastor's turn at the register the clerk was smiling and pleasant.

God's shalom isn't just a nice feeling we get when everything is going well for us. He is a Person who invades our hearts, setting things right and bringing us into the fullness of what God has for us. When we are submitted to His lordship in our lives, we are empowered to release His peace wherever we go. We have been sent on the same mission for which Jesus was sent—to release the ever-increasing kingdom of God, which is ruled by Sar Shalom, the Prince of Peace.

ENDNOTES

1. *Black's Law Dictionary Free Online Legal Dictionary 2nd Edition,* "What Is Natural Law?" Accessed on May 1, 2011, from http://thelawdictionary.org/natural-law/.

2. Andrew Murray, *God's Will: Our Dwelling Place* (New Kensington, PA: Whitaker House Publishers, 1991), 11-12.

3. George Whitefield, "Christ the only Preservative against a Reprobate Spirit," Reformed Sermon Archives, The Sermons of George Whitefield. Accessed on April 4, 2014, from http://reformedsermonarchives.com/whit34.htm.

CHAPTER 3

THE TEACHER OF PEACE

BY DR. JEN

THE FIRST CAUSE

The vast size of the universe is almost incomprehensible to the human mind. The tiny planet on which we live, a mere speck in space, is embedded within and surrounded by an unimaginably huge universe which is impossible to measure. In the past, scientists thought time and space were infinite. Based on astronomical evidence and recent discoveries, however, physicists now believe there is an outer boundary and there was a distinct beginning.

Although multitudes of scientists have spent their lives studying the mysteries of the creation of the universe, their theories are purely hypothetical. All suppositions about creation, however, can be reduced to two possibilities: (1) There is no creator; there is only a very long period of time and random evolutionary changes, or (2) there was "an uncaused First Cause that was 'outside' or transcendent to the universe."[1]

We know this First Cause to be our Creator God:

> *In the beginning God created the heavens and the earth* (Genesis 1:1).[2]

Although there were no *human* eyewitnesses at the time of creation, the Scriptures tell us that there were in fact witnesses to the events that took place. God, of course, witnessed the events of creation—Father, Son, and Holy Spirit. The Prince of Peace, Sar Shalom, spoke forth His command, "Shalom!" and everything came into order through the power of the Holy Spirit.

Jesus was the teacher of peace in a great object lesson about shalom at the time of creation. The will of God was released from heaven in a great rushing river of peace and God's will was instantly done, accomplishing the creation of all things. The Living Word spoke and the elements of the earth and universe immediately snapped and clicked and roared into perfect order. The voice like the sound of many waters spoke and the will of God was accomplished (see Rev 1:15). Chaos was conquered and the universe was formed.

> *In the beginning was the Word, and the Word was with God, and the Word was God. He was in the beginning with God. All things were made through Him, and without Him nothing was made that was made. In Him was life, and the life was the light of men* (John 1:1-4).

Shalom contains within it God's goodness, blessedness, and prosperity. When the work of creation was fully accomplished, all that had been created was pronounced good: *"And God saw everything that He had made, and behold, it was very good (suitable, pleasant) and He approved it completely"* (Gen. 1:31 AMP). *Good* is *tôv* in Hebrew, meaning good to the senses, pleasant, desirable, prosperous, fruitful, abundant, joyful, and favorable. The definition of *tôv* describes the qualities of that which would be created by shalom.

The time of creation and the laying of the foundation of the earth were visibly displayed to an innumerable company of angels. Even the stars themselves sang praise to God. Referring to this time, the Lord answered Job and said:

> *Where were you when I laid the foundation of the earth? Declare to Me, if you have and know understanding. Who determined the measures of the earth, if you know? Or who stretched the measuring line upon it? Upon what were the foundations of it fastened, or who laid its cornerstone, when the morning stars sang together and all the sons of God shouted for joy?* (Job 38:4-7 AMP).

GRAND UNIFICATION THEORY

The elements that make up the physical, or "temporal," universe consist of matter, energy, space, and time. How the elemental building blocks are connected with one another and how they are all "held together" into a unified whole has been a topic of much scientific investigation.

Physicists dream of finding a "Theory of Everything," or a Grand Unification Theory, which ties together all rules and hypotheses about the universe in one equation. In other words, what connects everything to everything else? What holds all things together? Even if physicists can break it down to a simplified equation and essential key particle, we still must answer the question of who delineated the rules of the universe and what force holds the particles together.

What if the Grand Unification Theory is not an equation but a *Person*? Scripture, in fact, tells us that it is Christ Himself who holds the universe together:

> *For it was in Him that all things were created, in heaven and on earth, things seen and things unseen, whether thrones, dominions, rulers, or authorities; all things were created and exist through Him [by His service, intervention] and in and for Him. And He Himself existed before all things, and in Him all things consist (cohere, are held together)* (Colossians 1:16-17 AMP).

The same Living Word who spoke the worlds into existence became part of His own physical creation in the fullness of time so humanity could come into a personal relationship with the Creator. Isaiah prophesied of the coming Savior:

> *Thus says God the Lord, who created the heavens and stretched them out, who spread forth the earth and that which comes from it, who gives breath to the people on it, and spirit to those who walk on it: "I, the Lord, have called You in righteousness, and will hold Your hand; I will keep You and give You as a covenant to the people, as a light to the Gentiles"* (Isaiah 42:5-6).

The kingdom of God held full sway over the earth until Adam and Eve sinned. Although God still holds the title deed, sin caused an invasion of evil to take place. Adam and Eve forfeited their dominion of the earth and a war between two kingdoms began—good versus evil, light versus darkness, love versus fear, peace versus chaos.

When Adam and Eve fell, chaos reentered the created universe. Nevertheless, the Living Word still speaks shalom and holds the universe together. If He ceased speaking His Word, the elements would fly apart and chaos would reign once more. In the last days, shalom will find its full expression (see Rev. 21-22).

> [But] in the last of these days He has spoken to us in [the person of a] Son, Whom He appointed Heir and lawful Owner of all things, also by and through Whom He created the worlds and the reaches of space and the ages of time [He made, produced, built, operated, and arranged them in order].... He is the perfect imprint and very image of [God's] nature, upholding and maintaining and guiding and propelling the universe by His mighty word of power (Hebrews 1:2-3 AMP).

The kingdom of God is still advancing on the earth today. Eventually God's kingdom will expand and fill the whole earth. Voices in heaven will shout with great rejoicing, *"The kingdoms of this world have become the kingdoms of our Lord and of His Christ, and He shall reign forever and ever!"* (Rev. 11:15). Shalom will swallow up all turmoil and disorder as the kingdom of God triumphs and the Lord once again pronounces everything under the authority of His kingdom "good."

The Book of Daniel tells about this ever-expanding kingdom:

> *While you were watching, a rock was cut out, but not*
> *by human hands.... The rock that struck the statue*
> *became a huge mountain and filled the whole earth....*
> *In the time of those kings, the God of heaven will set up*
> *a kingdom that will never be destroyed, nor will it be*
> *left to another people. It will crush all those kingdoms*
> *and bring them to an end, but it will itself endure*
> *forever* (Daniel 2:34-35, 44).

THE WILL OF GOD

Let us consider the blessedness contained in God's holy and perfect will. How perfect is heaven? What constitutes its glory? Heaven contains the fullness of God. There are no unfulfilled needs in heaven. The presence of Father God grants rest, rejoicing, and everlasting satisfaction to every inhabitant thereof. Because God's will reigns supreme, His goodness and blessing fill everyone and everything. Therefore, the inhabitants of heaven rejoice continually in the love and glory of God.

When God's kingdom comes to earth, the will of God is released on earth. The heavenly atmosphere of glory, love, and blessing is poured out on earth. Many Christians have a revelation of God's will as far as His plan for their individual lives. However, the will of God is so much more than a plan for an individual. God has an eternal purpose to redeem humanity and restore His kingdom. To this end He is always working.

Paul said that God has *"made known to us the mystery of His will, according to His good pleasure which He purposed in*

Himself" (Eph. 1:9). Abraham became part of what God was doing in the earth. It wasn't all about Abraham, however. It was about the eternal purposes of God being accomplished—the God-story, not the Abraham-story. Abraham did God's will, not his own.

> *If Abraham, by what he did for God, got God to approve him, then he could certainly have taken credit for it. But the story we're given is a God-story, not an Abraham-story. What we read in Scripture is, "Abraham entered into what God was doing..."* (Romans 4:2 MSG).

Jesus came to do the will of His Father on earth:

> *Jesus answered them, My Father has worked [even] until now, [He has never ceased working; He is still working] and I, too, must be at [divine] work* (John 5:17 AMP).

Jesus *chose* to submit His will fully to the will of His Father and finish the work that God had called Him to do. In doing the will of God, Jesus ate of the hidden manna, which gives life and strength to all who partake of it. This is why Jesus said to His disciples, *"My food is to do the will of Him who sent Me, and to finish His work"* (John 4:34). Who can eat this heavenly food? Those who do the will of the Father.

Because the will of God contains His pleasure, Jesus delighted in doing God's will (see Isa. 46:9-10; Eph. 1:5). We, too, can know the joy and blessing of yielding our will for the sake of entering into the purposes of God. How thrilled we should be that we have been given the opportunity to co-labor with God in prayer and in our actions as He works out His story on planet earth!

God's will is the full expression of His glory, love, goodness, and power to accomplish His intended purposes. All the inhabitants of heaven rejoice in the blessedness of the will of God working in unhindered manifestation. The first two human beings of creation, and all of creation itself, experienced heaven on earth because everything was in harmony with the will of God.

CO-LABORERS IN KINGDOM BUILDING

Jesus came to restore peace to the earth. He taught about His kingdom. He demonstrated His kingdom. The Lord created a "one accord" portal in an upper room and once again the mighty rushing sound of the will of God invading the earth in power was heard. A small group of believers was filled with the essence of heaven on that day. Jesus commissioned them and sent them forth as His ambassadors of God's will and His kingdom. And they *"turned the world upside down"* (Acts 17:6).

We, too, have been made ambassadors of Christ...if we are willing to accept the assignment given to us by God. Those who say yes to the Lord are the ones who are *"the called according to"* God's design and purpose (see Rom. 8:28). All things work together for good for those who love God and His will. They are those who *"seek first the kingdom of God and His righteousness"* (Matt. 6:33). God will spare no good thing for their sake. He will give them everything they need (see Matt. 6:25-34).

Paul said, *"We are assured and know that [God being a partner in their labor] all things work together and are [fitting into a plan] for good to and for those who love God and are called according to [His] design and purpose"* (Rom. 8:28 AMP).

How can we cooperate with the Prince of Peace in kingdom building? How do we submit to the lordship of Jesus Christ and God's will? To cooperate with God's will we must yield our will to His will. Every moment becomes an opportunity to practice yielding to God's will. We simply yield our will to Him and God works through us: *"It is God who works in you both to will and to do for His good pleasure"* (Phil. 2:13).

PATTERNS OF THE KINGDOM

Peace reconciles all things to God. When peace reigns, God reigns. When God reigns, peace, prosperity, and provision abound. Jesus's main mission on earth was to establish peace by expanding the kingdom of God, thus fulfilling Isaiah's prophecy of the Prince of Peace bringing an ever-increasing kingdom:

> *For unto us a Child is born, unto us a Son is given; and the government will be upon His shoulder. And His name will be called Wonderful, Counselor, Mighty God, Everlasting Father, Prince of Peace. Of the increase of His government and peace there will be no end, upon the throne of David and over His kingdom, to order it and establish it with judgment and justice from that time forward, even forever* (Isaiah 9:6-7).

Because the reign of shalom was so important to Jesus, before He ascended back to the Father He commissioned His disciples to be *ambassadors* of peace: *"Then He called His twelve disciples together and gave them power and authority over all demons, and to cure diseases. He sent them to preach the kingdom of God and to heal the sick"* (Luke 9:1-2). And not long after this, He appointed another 72 who were to represent Him, saying, *"And heal the sick there, and say to them, 'The kingdom of God has come near to you'"* (Luke 10:9).

The kingdom of God wasn't a concept newly introduced in the New Testament. In fact, there were many types, or pictures, of the kingdom of God throughout Scripture. In each of these cases, we will be able to see God's ultimate plan for shalom to rule and reign in the earth—wholeness and completeness, where nothing is missing and nothing is lacking.

How is God's will accomplished? How does He establish His kingdom? The Father wills, the Son speaks shalom, and the Holy Spirit works. The practical outworking of God's will bringing peace is accomplished through the Holy Spirit. Water is a type of the Holy Spirit throughout Scripture. Jesus said, *"Whoever believes in Me, as the Scripture has said, rivers of living water will flow from within them.' By this He meant the Spirit, whom those who believed in Him were later to receive"* (John 7:38-39 NIV).

The Garden of Eden

The first picture of the kingdom of shalom seen in the Bible is in the Garden of Eden. God spent six days creating the heavens, the earth, and everything in them. On the sixth day He came to the pinnacle of His creation: *"And the Lord God formed man of the dust of the ground, and breathed into his nostrils the breath of life; and man became a living being"* (Gen. 2:7).

In this perfect picture of God's creation, there was no sin, no disharmony, and nothing was missing or lacking for Adam or Eve or even in the creation itself. They were not aware of sin or shame, and He placed them in the Garden to tend and keep it, expanding it by exercising dominion over it. They lived in perfect harmony with creation, with one another, and with God Himself.

"A river went out of Eden to water the garden, and from there it parted and became four riverheads" (Gen. 2:10). It was one river that divided into streams that flowed to the four corners of the earth. What does this river represent? Psalms 46:4 proclaims, *"There is a river whose streams shall make glad the city of God, the holy place of the tabernacle of the Most High."* Ezekiel also had a vision of a river flowing from under the threshold of the temple of God that brought life and healing wherever it went (see Ezek. 47:1-12).

Jesus announced that He had living water to give those who are thirsty (see John 4:13-14), and that from whoever believed in Him, *"'rivers of living water will flow from within them.' By this He meant the Spirit, whom those who believed in Him were later to receive"* (John 7:38-39 NIV). Finally, Revelation 22:1-3 describes a river of the water of life *"proceeding from the throne of God and the Lamb."* The rivers in Genesis, therefore, symbolize the Holy Spirit, who goes forth to implement God's will.

God had granted Adam and Eve everything good to enjoy, but they were given just one command—they were warned not to eat from one tree in the middle of the Garden. The Bible says,

"And they heard the sound of the Lord God walking in the garden in the cool of the day" (Gen. 3:8), making it sound like a common experience for them to walk and talk with God. After they disobeyed God, however, they heard the familiar sound of His voice once again but they fled in terror.

Adam and Eve experienced prosperity, peace, righteousness, divine health, abundance, and perfect fellowship with all that was around them. There was nothing missing; there was perfect harmony in their relationships. It was just how God wanted them to live forever. However, we know that when sin entered the world, chaos was reintroduced into the story, thus fracturing the unity of all of creation.

The Wilderness

After the children of Israel had been in Egyptian bondage for more than 400 years, the day came when God heard their groaning and raised up Moses to deliver them. After they passed through the Red Sea on dry ground, they saw the Egyptian army behind them drowned in the sea, and they entered a time with God in the wilderness where God was their Source, providing for their needs over and over again.

When the people were hungry and wanted to return to Egypt, God heard their cries and gave them manna, which was sent from heaven every day (see Exod. 16). We even find a river of living water in the desert. When they were thirsty, God had Moses strike a rock and water gushed out to satisfy the thirst of over a million people and their livestock (see Exod. 17:1-7). Obviously it wasn't a little trickle. It was a mighty river pouring forth.

*For they drank from the spiritual Rock that traveled
with them, and that Rock was Christ* (1 Corinthians
10:4).

They were protected on every side, and blessed with perfect
health throughout the time they were in the wilderness. Is it
possible that the healing properties of the river from the rock
brought health to their bodies (see Ezek. 47:9)? Though they
spent 40 years wandering in the desert because of their sin, God
still worked to establish His kingdom among them, making sure
nothing was missing or lacking during that time. Their *"garments did not wear out"* and their feet did not *"swell these forty
years"* (Deut. 8:4). God was their Source, providing shalom on
their way to the Promised Land.

The Promised Land

When the children of Israel finally came to the Promised
Land, they entered a land that was marked by prosperity and
provision, a type of the kingdom of God. When Moses had previously sent the 12 spies to look at the land to make sure they
were able to take it, the spies brought back a cluster of grapes so
large that it had to be carried on a pole between two people, as
well as pomegranates and figs (see Num. 13:23). Unfortunately,
because of their sin and disobedience, that generation wandered
in the wilderness for 40 years and died without ever enjoying the
bounty of the land.

This verdant land was described as a land of tremendous fruitfulness, flowing with milk and honey. Author
Phillip Keller writes:

In the Scriptures the picture portrayed of the Promised Land, to which God tried so hard to lead Israel from Egypt, was that of a land flowing with milk and honey. Not only is this figurative language but also essentially scientific terminology. In agricultural terms we speak of a milk flow and a honey flow. By this we mean the peak season of spring and summer when pastures are at their most productive stages. The livestock that feed on the forage and the bees that visit the blossoms are said to be producing a corresponding flow of milk or honey. So a land flowing with milk and honey is a land of rich, green, luxuriant pastures.[3]

The Book of Deuteronomy consists of three speeches by Moses to the next generation of the children of Israel shortly before they were to enter the Promised Land, into which they were to be led by Joshua. Moses again reminded them of the abundance that existed there before they entered and exhorted them to keep their hearts faithful to God:

> *Therefore you shall keep the commandments of the Lord your God, to walk in His ways and to fear Him. For the Lord your God is bringing you into a good land, a land of brooks of water, of fountains and springs, that flow out of valleys and hills; a land of wheat and barley, of vines and fig trees and pomegranates, a land of olive oil and honey; a land in which you will eat bread without scarcity, in which you will lack nothing; a land whose stones are iron and out of whose hills you can dig copper. When you have eaten and are full, then you shall bless*

the Lord your God for the good land which He has given you (Deuteronomy 8:6-10).

The Book of Acts

On the day of Pentecost, a group of righteous Jews waiting in an upper room came into one accord with one another and aligned with heaven. Their unity opened a portal in the heavenly realm, permitting another outpost of heaven to be established on earth—in the hearts of individual believers. Shalom rushed in "like a mighty river" and glory like an "overflowing stream" (see Isa. 66:12). Living water was provided in great abundance! Likewise, when the glory of God filled Ezekiel's temple, it entered with the *"sound of many waters"* (Ezek. 43:2). And when the apostle John was caught up into heaven, he beheld the Lord Jesus Christ in all His glory and heard His voice *"as the sound of many waters"* (Rev. 1:15).

The early church preached and demonstrated the kingdom of God. When the early church first began gathering together, they had all things in common and they later laid their possessions at the feet of the apostles. They didn't give their goods to the government but practiced charity and generosity with one another in the church. God reigned among them. There was great joy and peace among the brethren, and they lived in the blessings of unity, generosity, miracles, and great glory. Acts 2:42-47 says of this time:

> *And they continued steadfastly in the apostles' doctrine and fellowship, in the breaking of bread, and in prayers. Then fear came upon every soul, and many wonders and signs were done through the apostles. Now all who*

believed were together, and had all things in common,
and sold their possessions and goods, and divided them
among all, as anyone had need. So continuing daily
with one accord in the temple, and breaking bread
from house to house, they ate their food with gladness
and simplicity of heart, praising God and having favor
with all the people.

In the beginning, God established a temple-garden in Eden in which He dwelt with His children. He was their God and they were His people. There was no need for sin offerings at first because there was no sin. After the fall, God prepared the nation of Israel to be His people and dwelt among them first in a tabernacle and then in a temple.

However, the day of Pentecost ushered in a new era. The early church displayed God's rule and reign in and through individuals. Now God was not confined to living in the *midst* of His people, He made *people* His dwelling place! His dwelling place multiplied from a physical location to the hearts of a multitude of believers. The Teacher of Peace no longer preached just in Israel, but His testimony would be preached through the mouths of believers around the world through the power of the Holy Spirit.

ENDNOTES

1. Institute for Creation Research, "Time, Space, and Matter," accessed on October 29, 2013, from http://www.icr.org/first-cause/.

2. The word translated created is the Hebrew word bara, which means open up, bring into tangible existence, or

create from nothing (see Gen. 1:1). Adam, on the other hand, was "made," from the Hebrew word asah, meaning to fashion, make, or produce. A second verb is used for the "shaping" of Adam, yatsar, meaning to fashion, make, produce, form as one would form pottery (see Gen. 1:26).

"Note also that 'create' (Hebrew bara) is used seven times in Genesis 1, never in Genesis 2–4. In that second account, 'made' and 'formed' (Hebrew asah, yatsar) are the words used. Genesis 2:3 stresses the fact that 'create' and 'make' are different, when it tells us that God rested 'from all his work which God created and made.' Evidently the verb 'create,' which always has the Creator as its subject, refers to His work in calling entities into existence; 'make' refers to systems constructed (by either God or men) out of previously created entities. The heavens and the earth were both 'created' and 'made.'" [H. Morris, "Created and made," Institute for Creation Research, accessed on April 5, 2014, from http://www.icr.org/article/5811/.]

3.   W. P. Keller, *A Shepherd Looks at Psalm 23* (Grand Rapids, MI: Zondervan, 2007), 54.

CHAPTER 4

THE KINGDOM OF SOLOMON

BY DR. JEN

SOLOMON'S KINGDOM

King David greatly desired it in his heart to build God a house in which He could dwell. But because he had been a man of war and had shed so much blood, God said that he wasn't the one to do it. God, therefore, commissioned Solomon to build the house for His name. David gave his son Solomon the heavenly blueprint for building the temple before he died, and Solomon accomplished the work of building a dwelling place for God. Prefiguring the outpouring on the day of Pentecost, at the dedication of the temple God answered the prayers of Solomon with a cloud of His glory—an outpouring of the Holy Spirit. Living water flowed into Solomon's kingdom and God's glory filled the temple (see 2 Chron. 7:1-3).

Perhaps the greatest picture of the kingdom is revealed in the kingdom of Solomon. Solomon became king of Judah after David died. The Bible sums up his reign as this: *"For he had dominion over all the region on this side of the River from Tiphsah even to Gaza, namely over all the kings on this side of the River; and he had peace on every side all around him. And Judah and Israel dwelt safely, each man under his vine and his fig tree, from Dan as far as Beersheba, all the days of Solomon"* (1 Kings 4:24-25).

We can see that the reign of Solomon in many ways typifies the kingdom of God established by Christ. David knew war. Solomon knew peace. The name *Solomon* in Hebrew is *Schlomo*, from the root word shalom, meaning peace. How fitting it was that Solomon experienced the very definition of shalom during his reign—he had peace on every side, it was an era of prosperity and safety for his people and him, and every man dwelled under his own vine and fig tree. That phrase helps us understand the kingdom of peace Jesus came to establish.

Under His Vine and Fig Tree

Micah speaks of the fig tree in reference to the coming of the kingdom. He says, *"They will hammer their swords into plowshares and their spears into pruning hooks; nation will not lift up sword against nation, and never again will they train for war. Each of them will sit under his vine and under his fig tree, with no one to make them afraid"* (Micah 4:3-4 NASB). To sit under the vine and fig tree is a metaphor for peace, prosperity, and safety, the very blessings that abound in the kingdom of God. Both the vine and fig tree were also used in Scripture to represent the nation of Israel.

We can see this same concept of sitting under the fig tree in the New Testament when Jesus called Nathanael to be His disciple. When Jesus saw Nathanael sitting under a fig tree, He recognized him as a man in whom there was no deceit. When Nathanael asked how Jesus knew him, He responded by saying, *"Before Philip called you, when you were under the fig tree, I saw you"* (John 1:48).

Philip implies Nathanael was well acquainted with the law and the prophets: *"We have found Him of whom Moses in the law, and also the prophets, wrote—Jesus of Nazareth, the son of Joseph"* (John 1:45). Some Bible scholars believe that Nathanael may have been meditating on the portion of Scripture in Genesis 28:9-11 about Jacob. Jacob was a trickster whose name was later changed to Israel. Jesus called Nathanael a man without guile and a true Israelite. Jacob dreamed of a ladder to heaven with angels ascending and descending. Jesus said Nathanael would see heaven open and angels ascending and descending upon Jesus Himself, the Son of Man in whose presence Nathanael was standing.

In that day, it was common to pray seated in the shade of a fig tree. It was common to offer prayers for the coming of the Messiah each time they prayed. Therefore, Nathanael's astonished reply to Jesus could have been because the Messiah revealed the meditations of his heart and had seen him praying for the Messiah to come. Nathanael understood that Jesus was a King who came to establish a kingdom: *"Rabbi, You are the Son of God! You are the King of Israel!"* (John 1:49).

The fig tree is also used as a type of the kingdom of God. Because Solomon's reign was one of shalom, each man could dwell securely and rest under his vine and fig tree. The leaves provided shade from the sun and the fruit was good for food and drink. There was no need to be constantly on the alert because there was peace in the land.

Jesus referenced the fig tree as foreshadowing the return of the kingdom:

> *Look at the fig tree, and all the trees. When they are already budding, you see and know for yourselves that summer is now near. So you also, when you see these things happening, know that the kingdom of God is near* (Luke 21:29-31).

At another time when Jesus was teaching, He alluded to the kingdom of Solomon, and then announced He is greater than Solomon (see Luke 11:31). The truth is, as great as Solomon's kingdom was, as much as it pictured the kingdom of peace in the end days, the fullness of the kingdom is yet to come. Solomon's kingdom came to an end; Jesus's kingdom is ever expanding. Solomon's kingdom was only a type and shadow of that which was to come, the one commanded by Jesus Christ.

Perhaps the greatest deficiency of Solomon's kingdom was not its inability to influence the world but the personal failures of Solomon himself. He allowed the world (through his many wives from different nations) to influence him to build high places to foreign gods. This turned his heart away from the true God of Israel, and it ultimately resulted in a divided kingdom.

Prosperity and Wealth in Solomon's Kingdom

Not only did Solomon have peace on every side, but there was also an abundance of wealth during his reign. When the shalom of God comes, it brings peace, provision, and great abundance into our lives. It sets things right, bringing harmony and restoration to every area.

During his reign, *"All King Solomon's drinking vessels were gold, and all the vessels of the House of the Forest of Lebanon were pure gold. Not one was silver, for this was accounted as nothing in the days of Solomon"* (1 Kings 10:21). His kingdom contained so much wealth that silver was almost worthless during his reign.

Solomon became greater than all the other kings of the earth, in both riches and wisdom: *"Now all the earth sought the presence of Solomon to hear his wisdom, which God had put in his heart. Each man brought his present: articles of silver and gold, garments, armor, spices, horses, and mules, at a set rate year by year"* (1 Kings 10:24-25). And not only that, but *"the king had merchant ships at sea with the fleet of Hiram. Once every three years the merchant ships came bringing gold, silver, ivory, apes, and monkeys"* (1 Kings 10:22).

King Solomon was a blessed man indeed. And as that was only a type and shadow of what was to come, that means the kingdom of shalom will bring many of the same blessings as Jesus reigns in our lives. Isaiah prophesied of the material prosperity inherent in the coming kingdom:

> *The abundance of the sea shall be turned to you, the wealth of the Gentiles shall come to you. The multitude of camels shall cover your land, the dromedaries*

of Midian and Ephah; all those from Sheba shall come; they shall bring gold and incense, and they shall proclaim the praises of the Lord.... Therefore your gates shall be open continually; they shall not be shut day or night, that men may bring to you the wealth of the Gentiles, and their kings in procession.... Instead of bronze I will bring gold, instead of iron I will bring silver, instead of wood, bronze, and instead of stones, iron. I will also make your officers peace, and your magistrates righteousness (Isaiah 60:5-6, 11, 17).

ATTRIBUTES OF THE KINGDOM

When the Prince of Peace establishes His kingdom in our hearts and lives, we experience prosperity, joy, divine health, and divine order in great measure. Though we see a foretaste now, a time is coming when peace will abound and the fullness of the kingdom will manifest.

Isaiah prophesied of a time when God would *"extend peace"* to Jerusalem *"like a river"* (Isa. 66:12), and that the people would *"hammer their swords into plowshares and their spears into pruning hooks. Nation will not lift up sword against nation, and never again will they learn war"* (Isa. 2:4 NASB).

When the kingdom of God comes, His peace invades all areas of life. Relationships are restored, war ceases, and joy is full. The fullness of the kingdom of God and His peace includes everything—even the animals, the weather, and all else in the physical realm—that has not known peace since the fall of man. Someday the lion and the lamb will dwell together in peace (see

Isa. 11:6-9) because the Lord even makes a covenant with the beasts of the field (see Hos. 2:18).

Occasionally, when I (Dennis) am praying on our deck, tiny finches and other birds land on my legs and rest there until I finally have to get up. It may be a coincidence, but it reminds me of St. Francis, the patron saint of animals. St. Francis of Assisi (1181/1182-1226) was an Italian friar and preacher who embraced poverty, humility, and simplicity of life. He founded the Franciscan order, or Order of Friars Minor. His rule of life for his followers was: "To follow the teachings of our Lord Jesus Christ and to walk in His footsteps." St. Francis had a remarkable way with animals following his revelation that the gospel was for all the creatures of God. On one occasion, he walked into the midst of a flock of birds and began preaching to them.

> St Francis lifted up his eyes, and saw on some trees by the wayside a great multitude of birds; and being much surprised, he said to his companions, "Wait for me here by the way, whilst I go and preach to my little sisters the birds"; and entering into the field, he began to preach to the birds which were on the ground, and suddenly all those also on the trees came round him, and all listened while St Francis preached to them, and did not fly away until he had given them his blessing.... As he said these words, all the birds began to open their beaks, to stretch their necks, to spread their wings and reverently to bow their heads to the ground, endeavouring by their motions and by their songs to

manifest their joy to St Francis. And the saint rejoiced with them.[1]

And on another occasion:

It is reported that, when St. Francis lived in the city of Gubbio, a ferocious wolf terrorized the citizenry. St. Francis bent his steps alone toward the spot where the wolf was known to be, while many people followed at a distance, and witnessed the miracle. The wolf, seeing all this multitude, ran towards St. Francis with his jaws wide open. As he approached, the saint, making the sign of the cross, cried out: "Come hither, brother wolf; I command thee, in the name of Christ, neither to harm me nor anybody else." Marvellous to tell, no sooner had St. Francis made the sign of the cross, than the terrible wolf, closing his jaws, stopped running, and coming up to St. Francis, lay down at his feet as meekly as a lamb.[2]

These miracles may seem quite amazing, but they are sign-posts pointing to the day prophesied by Isaiah when the lion will lie down with the lamb (see Isa. 11:5-9). Why would it seem surprising that animals can respond to the peace of God? It is well known that animals can sense human emotion. Horses become skittish when their rider is afraid. Yellow jackets are stirred up to attack when they sense fear. Tracking dogs can pick up the scent of emotions. How much more, then, should they be aware of the supernatural peace of God!

In every place where the kingdom of God manifests, blessing and order follow close behind. Because shalom includes wholeness and health, healing occurs when God's peace comes. Illness wasn't part of God's original plan in the Garden. Sickness came only after sin entered. God promised Israel that He would keep the diseases and infirmities that plagued the Egyptians away from them if they would obey Him.

> *You shall be blessed above all peoples; there shall not be a male or female barren among you or among your livestock. And the Lord will take away from you all sickness, and will afflict you with none of the terrible diseases of Egypt which you have known, but will lay them on all those who hate you* (Deuteronomy 7:14-15).

Protection from sickness and disease would have continued had the people remained obedient to the commandments of God. As has already been discussed, each miracle of healing Jesus performed was shalom breaking into the earthly realm. When peace comes, there God's order is restored (see Isa. 65:19-25).

FOUR ELEMENTS TO LIVING IN GOD'S KINGDOM OF PEACE

Each of us are called to walk in more peace than what we're currently experiencing. We may understand the message of peace, but until we begin to walk in it on a daily basis, then we're not living enough of it. As long as we have anxiety and stress in our lives, then we have not entered into what God has made available for us. Here are four elements we must understand to experience this kingdom of peace in the way God intended.

Vision

We can't have something we can't see. When Nicodemus came to Jesus, Jesus made two distinctions about the kingdom of God (see John 3:1-3). First, Jesus said that one must be born again to *see* the kingdom. Now, many believers are born again and have no understanding of the kingdom, but they have the spiritual capacity to understand the kingdom of God nonetheless. We must first have a vision of the kingdom before we can enter it.

Second, Jesus said that it was possible to *enter* the kingdom. We must know the kingdom is "at hand," and we can appropriate what God has made available for us. Walking in the shalom of God is possible for us now; we can tap into the fruit of the Spirit now. This is not for some far-off day in the future.

Many individuals have been believers for years but live in constant anxiety, anger, or stress. If we have anxiety, anger, and stress, then we're not really *living* in the kingdom of God. The evidence of the kingdom is peace. Jesus has given us the gift of peace so it is always available for us. We don't lose our salvation when we lose our peace, but we are not dwelling in the realm of the kingdom because Jesus is not ruling in our heart. If we learn to practice a lifestyle of forgiveness, we can begin to live in supernatural peace.

The kingdom of God was, is, and is yet to come. We look back to see what God has already provided for us, we pursue the things of the kingdom for today, and we look toward the future fullness.

Not only do we need to take advantage of what we *already* know, we should catch the vision of those things coming in the future, lay hold of them by faith, and bring them into the present. Yes, there is plenty more available down the road, but if we don't enter into what God is doing now, we will miss it. We must first see the availability of the shalom of God. Then we must practice a forgiveness lifestyle to stay in peace.

The Pursuit of Wholeness

We should be intentional about our sanctification. We must stop waiting until we are in a difficult or hostile situation before trying to practice peace. Instead, we must deal with our flesh on a moment-by-moment basis and be prepared in advance for when trouble strikes. How can we run a marathon without training for it?

We should get ahead of the devil, the world, and our flesh by intentionally allowing God to search our hearts on a regular basis. The Lord knows what is coming in the future, and He will prepare us to be victorious if we let Him. Our prayer must be, "Lord, You know what I will face today. Show me any hidden 'triggers' in my heart that need to be uprooted so I can respond in a godly way instead of reacting in carnality." That's *intentional sanctification*, the result of which will be a life of peace and wholeness.

> *If you have run with the footmen, and they have wearied you, then how can you contend with horses? And if in the land of peace, in which you trusted, they*

*wearied you, then how will you do in the floodplain of
the Jordan?* (Jeremiah 12:5)

What does Jesus give us to replace our pain, fear, or anger
so we can be whole? Peace. When Jesus washes away our pain
and our sorrow through forgiveness, we feel peace in our heart.
A supernatural exchange takes place.

The Sacrifice of Obedience

Too many believers continue to walk in the flesh even after
they learn how to tap into the fruit of the Spirit. We are called
to be zealous followers of Christ, and He is leading us forth
into kingdom living. Once we know how to stay in peace, we
are responsible to make a serious effort to live there. God wants
our obedience, not our casual Christianity. Real Christianity
requires discipline: prayer, reading the Bible, godly conduct,
learning to abide in Christ, laying down carnal weapons, and letting peace *"guard our hearts and our minds"* (Phil. 4:7).

There is an element of risk when we trust God to keep us
safe. In hostile situations, the majority of believers "put up a
wall." That is a carnal weapon, but many of us have never learned
to trust God to keep us safe. Instead of putting up a wall with
willpower, we can simply yield to God in our heart. It is just a
matter of trusting and yielding to Him. We will feel supernatural peace. Although we may feel vulnerable without that wall,
nothing can get through God's peace.

*The peace of God, which surpasses all understanding,
will guard your hearts and minds through Christ Jesus*
(Philippians 4:7).

We can't enjoy the safety of shalom unless we risk our flesh and yield to God. When we reason, when we try, and when we defend ourselves, we lose shalom and enter into the realm of chaos. When we risk, trust, and yield to the Lord, however, we enter into shalom. That's the sacrifice of obedience.

Fulfillment

We can't receive something we are not open to and we can't give something we haven't received. Without the fruit of peace in our lives, we have dead religion. Jesus is expanding His kingdom of shalom and He is inviting us to be a part of it. Abraham entered into what God was doing, and God became his inheritance—his *"exceedingly great reward"* (Gen. 15:1).

The members of the faithful Zadok priesthood who didn't "go astray" in their hearts received God Himself as their inheritance:

> But the priests, the Levites, the sons of Zadok, who kept charge of My sanctuary when the children of Israel went astray from Me, they shall come near Me to minister to Me.... It shall be, in regard to their inheritance, that I am their inheritance (Ezekiel 44:15, 28).

Those who faithfully pursue God's kingdom of shalom find a fulfillment and satisfaction in God unknown to casual Christians. We find God, and in the process He exchanges our anxiety for His peace, our disorder for His order, our emptiness for His fullness.

Jesus preached the gospel of the kingdom and declared that the time of the kingdom was *at hand*. "At hand" means near to us, close enough to touch. We only have to reach out and receive it, choose to live in it, and then allow it to expand in our life. We require vision, we need to pursue wholeness, and we must offer to God the sacrifice of obedience, but the fulfillment is available for all who desire it.

LOOKING FOR PEACEMAKERS

God has come to establish His kingdom of peace, and He has invited each of us to share in that kingdom, thus extending His rule and reign in the earth. Jesus said, *"Blessed are the peacemakers, for they shall be called sons of God"* (Matt. 5:9). Are you willing to be a person who brings peace to every situation you encounter? Are you willing to see God's kingdom come in the midst of your life? Are you willing, like Abraham, to become part of the God-story? God is looking for peacemakers!

ENDNOTES

1.   Ungolino di Monte Santa Maria (Author), W. Heywood (Translator), M. L'Engle (Introduction), *The Little Flowers of St. Francis of Assisi* (New York: A Vintage Spiritual Classics Original, May 1998, First Edition, Random House, Inc.), 36-37.

2.   Ibid., 47.

PART II

SUPERNATURAL POWER PEACE

CHAPTER 5

SUPERNATURAL POWER PEACE

BY DENNIS

DIFFERENT MANIFESTATIONS OF PEACE

Jennifer and I always spend our time with the Lord together, mostly sitting quietly in His presence, letting His peace fill us, guard us, and guide us. We love to meet with the Lord, dropping down into our spirits in order to experience all God has for us each day.

The Lord offers us a "daily portion" of Himself for our spiritual nourishment. The "daily bread" we request in the Lord's Prayer does not refer to our physical necessities so much as our spiritual needs. The majority of our time together is spent absorbing His peace—we very rarely talk during this time. We don't just preach about living a lifestyle of 24/7 peace, but we also long to actually experience it in a very real way.

One morning we were sitting quietly before the Lord, yielding to His presence and to one another. Just as we can open our hearts to God, we can open our hearts to include others (see 2 Cor. 6:11). After we had been lost in prayer for about an hour, the presence of Jesus Himself manifested in a powerful way. He was truly in the room with us! Peace that was full of glory permeated the atmosphere. We were immersed in peace that was saturated with the *power* of God. We both gasped and blurted out similar Scriptures at almost the same time. Jen exclaimed, "This is 'one accord.' This is what was happening in the upper room!" (see Acts 1:14). At almost the same time, I quoted the Scripture, *"If two of you agree...where two or three are gathered together in My name, there am I in the midst of them"* (Matt. 18:19-20). Jesus was there in our midst. A deep unity was taking place in that moment—we felt one with God and one with each other. It was not theoretical unity but the *experience* of unity.[1]

Since that time, when Jen and I have ministered together in different meetings, we've experienced this deep peace and unity in profound ways. After that experience of oneness, on a regular basis we would experience various manifestations of the unity of God's presence, and it would affect each group of people in a different way. We would pray for people, they would experience the presence of God, and later they would tell us about how their hearts were suddenly knit together with their church leaders. Married couples came with tears in their eyes, asking us to pray for them so that they would be knit together in unity. Some people would say that the atmosphere felt as thick as honey and they felt a sense of connection with everyone present at the meeting. The common denominator in all these meetings was the dual presence of deep peace and a sense of unity.

At other times, the presence of God would manifest as a corporate anointing and people would get saved sovereignly, others would be delivered from demonic influence, but all would later testify that God had been speaking the same thing to them all. We remember a particular meeting in a church in Massachusetts where the weight of God's presence came down, and miracles started taking place all over the sanctuary. There were emotional healings, physical healings, and words of knowledge given as people were set free from bondages that had afflicted them for years. Then we'd go somewhere else and God's presence would show up with a similar feeling, but it would be an altogether different manifestation in the hearts and lives of the people present.

After ministering for years and seeing the presence of God show up and move in these different ways, we now understand that all these were expressions of God's peace. Even unity is shalom expressed as "no walls or separation between us." This is why we call this *supernatural power peace*—it isn't the type of peace that we get from the world or even congenial Christian times of fellowship. This shalom releases the power of God. Whenever God shows up, the essence of who He is shows up with Him, setting all things right. When we talk about the shalom of God, we're talking about all of who He is showing up, bringing physical and emotional healing, deliverance, salvation, and causing hearts to be knit together in unity.

There are many different manifestations of God's presence, but they all have the common denominator of shalom. Shalom may be expressed in various ways such as healing, comfort, or unity. However, when the Lord shows up, things become complete and whole, things are set right, and there is nothing missing or lacking. The peace that Jesus gives is the embodiment of *full* salvation—total healing for the total man: body, soul, and spirit. Everything that we need is found in Christ alone.

ABUNDANCE BEGINS WITH INVESTMENT

Not long ago, as I was preparing to preach to our congregation, the Lord spoke a word to my spirit that has stuck with me ever since. That word is *abundance*. We see throughout the Scriptures that God is a God of abundance. At the core of abundance, however, is the presence of shalom. When God's shalom manifests through His presence, there is an abundance of anything we could ever want or need from God. That is why, when God's supernatural peace shows up at our meetings, it often ministers in many different ways depending on what He wants to do in a certain church and particular people present there.

However, there can be no abundance without investment on our end. What do I mean by this? Unless there's an investment into something, there will be no reaping. Any farmer will tell you that they won't have an abundant crop if they don't plant much in the soil. We cannot expect to get a harvest when we haven't planted anything in the ground.

The concept of sowing and reaping is a significant principle, or kingdom law. When Paul wrote to the Corinthian church, he referred to sowing spiritually but reaping material things: *"If we have sown spiritual things for you, is it a great thing if we reap your material things? If others are partakers of this right over you, are we not even more?"* (1 Cor. 9:11-12). Paul understood that sowing into the people spiritual things should cause him to reap some material benefits. Those who preach the gospel should receive monetary compensation. Otherwise, no one in ministry could provide food or shelter for themselves and their families.

We have even heard individuals say they are offended when Christian ministers receive honorariums and don't give all their books and CDs away for free, citing Matthew 10:8 as justification for their position: *"freely you have received, freely give."* However, when you read that section of Scripture in context, it actually says to freely minister spiritual things, but the worker is worthy to earn a living.

> *And as you go, preach, saying, "The kingdom of heaven is at hand." Heal the sick, cleanse the lepers, raise the dead, cast out demons. Freely you have received, freely give. Provide neither gold nor silver nor copper in your money belts, nor bag for your journey, nor two tunics, nor sandals, nor staffs; for a worker is worthy of his food* (Matthew 10:7-10).

In another place, when Paul was talking about sowing spiritual things, he tells the Galatians, *"Do not be deceived, God is not mocked; for whatever a man sows, that he will also reap"* (Gal. 6:7). As we travel throughout the churches, we have seen a lot of people who have tried to get something from God without investing anything into Him or His servants. As we can see from the scriptural references above, we are going to reap in proportion to what we have sowed. We cannot live a life of stinginess and expect to receive an abundant blessing from God.

However, where there is great investment there is great reward. There was a woman who heard we were ministering in Connecticut, so she got a babysitter for her children, took a ferry off the island on which she lived, and drove a number of hours to come to the meeting and receive from the Lord. She was willing to invest to receive a breakthrough. She was willing to pay a price. And the minute she showed up to the meeting, God met her and powerfully changed her life. But she first invested herself with her whole heart into what God was doing.

Sowing reveals what is important to us. Scripture tells us that our heart will always be where we invest our treasure (see Luke 12:34). If we sow our time, treasure, and talent into material possessions, entertainment, and vacations, our heart is there (not that those things are bad in and of themselves). When we sow regularly into someone's ministry, a church, or missions, our heart is likewise there. If we sow an offering to God because we are grateful for what He has done for us, the condition of our heart is revealed. The truth is that *all* we have belongs to Him. When it comes to giving to the Lord, we ask Him to tell us how much He wants us to *give back* to Him.

Without the investment of our time, talent, and treasure, we will not experience the shalom of God fully operative in our lives. By no means am I saying that we only do things to get God to respond to us—that is the wrong heart motive. But we will invest into what is important to us.

A SELFISH MINDSET

The sad fact is that we've seen a reversal of this principle of sowing and reaping in the body of Christ over the past years. Instead of Christians investing in order to get something from God, we find they often want God to give them things for free at the expense of someone else. Please don't get me wrong here—salvation is a free gift based on the work of Christ alone. However, God wants us to honor Him, honor His delegated authority, and honor one another.

If we get bent out of shape when we don't get the gifts or blessings someone else has, we have the covetous attitude that God owes us something He gave to another. God doesn't owe us anything at all. Everything in the Christian life is not free. Until that selfish mindset changes within us, there is not going to be a great harvest of the spiritual fruit of peace in the body of Christ, as God desires. We have to repent of our selfishness and begin to invest in peace.

Furthermore, there has been an infiltration of an "entitlement mentality" within the body of Christ. Many believe that someone else is required to take care of them and do for them what they should do for themselves. They don't take responsibility for investing into their own future. But God calls us to steward what we've been given. Sowing is an important part of stewardship.

In order for us to regularly experience the peace of God and especially the fullness of that peace, we must be people who invest into God and His plans and purposes. There is a reason why antidepressant and anti-anxiety medications are among the most frequently prescribed medications on the market today. Everyone wants to experience some sort of peace, some relief from their troubles, or at least have some of their relationships set right. So instead of investing in God and turning to Him, they invest in medications, drugs, and alcohol. They want to experience just a touch of peace, a moment of relief. We are not against doctors or medication. We are just trying to point out that if we don't spend the time investing into God, then we're not going to experience a peace lifestyle in a deep way.

The peace of God is available to us when we offer our emotions to Him and yield to the fruit of the Spirit. We experience peace in prayer when we open our heart to God in communion. We abide in peace when we walk in the Spirit, maintaining our spiritual connection in everyday life. The fullness of peace can only be known, however, by investing into His kingdom. We must invest in Him with all of our heart if we really want to walk in the fullness of God (see Jer. 29:13). If we don't invest, then there's little shalom for us.

THE ABUNDANCE OF THE WIDOW'S OIL

Second Kings 4 tells the story of a widow who came to Elisha asking for wisdom because she didn't know what to do. Her husband had just died, but he owed some people money. In those days, the creditor would take away the sons of a dead man who owed money so they could work off the father's debt. If this happened, the widow would have no way to provide for herself. This was an extremely desperate situation in which the widow found herself.

Elisha asked her what she had remaining in her house. The woman replied, *"Your maidservant has nothing in the house but a jar of oil"* (2 Kings 4:2). Then Elisha replied, *"Go, borrow vessels from everywhere, from all your neighbors—empty vessels; do not gather just a few. And when you have come in, you shall shut the door behind you and your sons; then pour it into all those vessels, and set aside the full ones"* (2 Kings 4:3-4).

The widow went home and did just as Elisha had told her to do. She began filling up the empty vessels, and when she asked her sons for another vessel to pour oil into, they said there were no more. And when there were no more vessels, then the oil stopped flowing. Once all of the vessels were full, Elisha said, *"Go, sell the oil and pay your debt; and you and your sons live on the rest"* (2 Kings 4:7).

Experiencing the abundance of God must start with an investment. Elisha could have waved his hand and produced a miracle another way—something instantaneous. But he didn't. He understood the power of investment, the principle of sowing and reaping. So many in the body of Christ today want instant peace, instant deliverance, and to instantly experience the presence of God. But God doesn't work that way. We must sow into the kingdom of God in order to reap the benefits thereof. Reaping abundance comes because we've sowed even during our times of lack.

AN EXAMPLE FROM MALACHI

A great example of sowing is found in the Book of Malachi. The people were robbing God by not bringing all the tithes and offerings into the storehouses. God explained the ramifications of their actions to the Israelites:

> *"Bring all the tithes into the storehouse, that there may be food in My house, and try Me now in this," says the Lord of hosts, "if I will not open for you the windows of heaven and pour out for you such blessing that there will not be room enough to receive it. And I will rebuke the devourer for your sakes, so that he will not destroy the fruit of your ground, nor shall the vine fail to bear fruit for you in the field"* (Malachi 3:10-11).

God wanted an investment so they could experience His abundance. He didn't promise to reward them with abundance despite bad behavior and a bad attitude. Malachi said that if Israel would invest into the kingdom of God, then He would do three things for them. First, God said that He would make sure there was always food in His house, which means there would be more than enough resources to fulfill the work of ministry. If we invest into God's kingdom, there will be an abundance of resources for the work of God.

Second, God said that He would open the windows of heaven over them and pour out a blessing they couldn't contain. Now this doesn't just involve finances, although they are included. Rather, God is saying that if we will sow into Him, then He will cause an open heaven so we will experience His abundance in our everyday lives. We will be candidates to experience the kingdom of shalom, because when He rules over us He blesses us.

Third, God promised the children of Israel that He would rebuke the devourer when they invested in the kingdom of God.

When we rob God, we rob ourselves of an abundant and fruitful life. We see too many believers who create their own troubles because they fail to sow properly.

In the New Testament, Jesus promises us much the same thing: *"I have come that they may have life, and that they may have it more abundantly"* (John 10:10). Jesus came so that nothing would be missing in our lives, everything would be complete and whole. Jesus wasn't promising that we would just have a great spiritual life or that we would just have money or that we would just be saved from hell. He was promising us an abundant *life*, meaning we would have everything that shalom contains.

THE WIDOW CONTINUED

The widow only had a jar of oil in the house—nothing more. How could God use that? We don't have to have major resources or many hours to sow into the kingdom of God. All we have to do is to use what we've been given. A poor widow in the New Testament only put a little bit of money in the offering, but Jesus said she had great riches laid up in heaven for the very reason that she did give out of her poverty (see Luke 21:1-4).

When Elisha asked the widow to get some vessels, she didn't only get a few. She had great faith and knew that in order to pay off the debt, she had to have a lot of money. The woman was able to sell the abundance of oil she received and pay off all her debt, keeping her family intact. Not only that, but she and her two sons were able to live off the rest of the money. That is faith. That is shalom. That is abundance. She invested and there was provision to meet her needs.

God honors the generosity of your heart and the extent of your faith. He has given you a capacity to experience Him (and it's much greater than what you're currently walking in), so the question is, "To what degree do you want to walk in fullness and abundance?"

THE SHUNAMMITE'S SON

In 2 Kings 4, we also read the story of a Shunammite woman who invested into the kingdom of God. Elisha would pass through the city quite often, so one day she and her husband decided to build him a little room upstairs so that when he passed by, he would have a place to stay. She invested in him by providing him with food and building a place for him to rest. What a wonderful example of honoring the man of God.

Her heart's desire was to have a son. Over time God blessed her and she conceived, giving birth to a son. Years later, while her son was working with his father in the field, he was stricken with a headache. So he went back home to his mother, where he died. The woman was understandably distraught, wondering why she would have a son only to have him die a short time later.

> *And so she departed, and went to the man of God at Mount Carmel. So it was, when the man of God saw her afar off, that he said to his servant Gehazi, "Look, the Shunammite woman! Please run now to meet her, and say to her, 'Is it well with you? Is it well with your husband? Is it well with the child?'" And she answered, "It is well." Now when she came to the man of God at the hill, she caught him by the feet, but Gehazi came*

near to push her away. But the man of God said, "Let
her alone; for her soul is in deep distress, and the Lord
has hidden it from me, and has not told me" (2 Kings
4:25-27).

Finding out what happened, Elisha sent his servant Gehazi
ahead of him to raise the child back to life. But he returned to
Elisha and told him that the child was dead. So Elisha went and
laid on top of him, bringing the boy back to life again. As amazing as that story is, it isn't the best part of the story. The best part
of the story is told a few chapters later.

Later, in 2 Kings 8, Elisha warned the Shunammite woman
that a famine was coming to the land. So she and her household
left the city and went to live in the land of the Philistines for
seven years. At the end of that time, the Shunammite returned
to Israel. When she went to appeal to the king for her house and
her land, much to her surprise, Gehazi, the servant of Elisha, was
there at that very moment telling the king of all the great things
Elisha had done. She and her son walked in and Gehazi said in
astonishment, *"My lord, O king, this is the woman, and this is her*
son whom Elisha restored to life." The king immediately directed
one of his officers, saying, *"Restore all that was hers, and all the*
proceeds of the field from the day that she left the land until now"
(2 Kings 8:1-6).

The Shunammite didn't just have her son restored back to
life, but she received the restoration of everything lost during
the seven years she was gone. She received back seven years' salary she couldn't earn because she was living in another country.
She got restoration. But more than restoration, she received

abundance. And nowhere do we find abundance manifested apart from shalom.

INWARD PEACE FIRST

We don't need the kind of peace the world gives; we need the peace that comes from above—supernatural power peace. That peace gives us shalom with ourselves, in our relationship with God, and in our relationships with the people around us.

We won't experience outward abundance until we have the inward abundance of shalom. When peace rules, Jesus rules. When Jesus rules, we have kingdom shalom. The very nature of shalom releases abundance, overflow, and restoration. But we must first invest into the kingdom. The nature of supernatural power peace is that it releases supernatural abundance.

PRACTICE

How to Sow

Many years ago, I (Jen) had something valuable stolen from me. Dennis was praying with me and told me to release what had been stolen as a gift to the person. He said, "No one can steal something from you if you give it to them as a gift." I closed my eyes in prayer and, as I released it to them from my heart, I suddenly saw a translucent golden shimmering "river" of anointing ascending from my hands, and the gift became part of that river. It flowed up to heaven where it multiplied and then flowed back down to me.

There are two important points: First, only that which enters the river of anointing counts as treasure laid up in heaven.

Whatever we sow must be accompanied by an anointed flow from our heart or it has no spiritual value. Second, as long as we keep sowing, the river continues to flow and our harvest continually increases. If we stop sowing, however, we cut off the river and it dries up.

ENDNOTE

1. The word agree in the Greek, sumphoneo, does not mean mental assent. It comes from sum, "together," and phoneo, "sound." Sumphoneo means to sound together, to be in harmony. The English word symphony is derived from sumphoneo. Even in the natural, the hearts of people make connections in relationships. A mother and infant make a real emotional connection that scientist call a "limbic loop." The same is true for a husband and wife who are in love with one another and close friends who genuinely care for one another. To a lesser degree, simply living together affects us emotionally and physically.

   In the realm of the spirit, God knits hearts together in spiritual relationships by the "bond of shalom" (see Eph. 4:3). God brings us together with certain people who are divine appointments. Divine appointments may be arranged by God to accomplish only one specific assignment or to become divine connections. When a fellowship of believers (two or more) comes into divine order leading to unity, God can release His divine purpose through them. When the bond between two or more individuals becomes strong enough for biblical unity to take place, they enter into one accord. God created us with the capacity for close relationship, and His ultimate goal is unity.

However, even in the natural, synchronization also occurs on other levels. Our emotions also affect others. "Human emotions are highly contagious. Seeing others' emotional expressions such as smiles often trigger the corresponding emotional response in the observer. Researchers have now found that feeling strong emotions makes different individuals' brain activity literally synchronous." If natural human emotions have such a strong effect on others, how much more powerful the supernatural emotions of the love and peace of God are. [Aalto University, "Synchronized brains: Feeling strong emotions makes people's brains 'tick together,'" Science Daily, May 24, 2012. Accessed on August 7, 2012, from http://www.sciencedaily.com/releases/2012/05/120524112342.htm.]

CHAPTER 6

POWER PEACE IS KINGDOM PEACE

BY DR. JEN

PEACE RULES

Dennis and I were traveling with a group of pastors in Canada some time ago, and we were in transit somewhere between two different provinces. Because it was quite a long distance to go in one day, we stopped about halfway through the trip to spend the night. We had been asked to have dinner and participate in a small house meeting afterward.

After the meeting was underway, a Micmac Indian woman suddenly had an emotional meltdown, wailing, "It's so much. My whole life—I want more of God—but my whole life, it's just too much! You don't understand!"

The other pastors in the room immediately called us over to minister to this woman. Dennis said to her, "Just calm down.

It's okay. We are going to go through just one thing at a time. It is all right. Now, just one at a time. People may not understand, but Jesus understands what you're going through. What is the first person or situation you see? Just stay focused on the first one that comes to mind. As soon as you get peace on that one, we'll deal with the next."

Dennis and I then prayed her through five major traumas—being physically beaten as a child, sexual molestation, having three abortions, being raped, and seeing her son murdered right before her eyes on the reservation. We led her through prayer, and she experienced peace each time before going any further. In just under 20 minutes, she was not only at peace, but she was actually joyful to be experiencing so much freedom! She exclaimed, "I feel the peace of God all around me, keeping me safe!" The experience of the peace of God guarding her became her reality.

Then she said to us, "Teach me how to do this. Explain to me what you did because I have to take this with me. I want to know how to help all those other hurting people on the reservation." So we gave her a mini-class right then and there. She left the meeting later with a glow on her face and a package of how-to training materials in her hand. There is nothing that can compare to the joy of helping people who are ignited with a passion to bring healing to others.

The kingdom of peace came to rule in her heart, setting things right and putting her emotions back in order. She experienced what Paul wrote to the Colossians, *"And let the peace of God rule in your hearts, to which also you were called in one body; and be thankful"* (Col. 3:15). The kingdom of peace set up its rule in her heart, establishing dominion and authority in her life.

THE KINGDOM OF PEACE

The Book of Genesis tells the story of Abraham meeting a great man named Melchizedek on his way home from battling other kings, and Abraham gave him a tenth of all that he owned. The writer of Hebrews sheds a little more light on this mystical character, who seems to have no beginning or end and no genealogy whatsoever. Melchizedek is Jesus, our great High Priest, as Hebrews points out, and he is a king of peace (see Heb. 7:2). If he is a king of peace, then this kingship is demonstrated through a dominion of peace, ultimately pointing to Jesus being the King of Peace.

A kingdom doesn't consist in what we do or the actions we perform, as Paul points out, *"but* [in] *righteousness and peace and joy in the Holy Spirit"* (Rom. 14:17). When the King of Peace is reigning in our hearts, we are governed by righteousness, peace, and joy in the Holy Spirit. Those are all attributes of supernatural power peace. As we submit ourselves to the lordship of Jesus Christ, everything contained in the shalom of God will flow toward us and through us.

Peace that pervades the kingdom governs our hearts and our lives—it acts as an umpire in everything we do. This is why Isaiah said that Jesus is the Prince of Peace (see Isa. 9:6). God establishes His government of peace in our hearts through His shalom, where we experience salvation, healing, prosperity, increase, deliverance, and everything is whole and set right in our lives. It is total healing for the total man: *"Now may the God of peace Himself sanctify you completely; and may your whole spirit, soul, and body be preserved blameless at the coming of our Lord Jesus Christ"* (1 Thess. 5:23).

Jesus doesn't increase His peace in our lives unless He first increases His government in our hearts. Colossians 3:15 says, *"Let the peace of God rule in your hearts."* Our level of peace reveals the extent of His government. For us to mature in God and in the power of His Spirit we must be people who are under the government of His peace. As His rule and reign increase through submission to His lordship, shalom will increase in all that we do, governing all of our decisions, guarding our hearts and minds, and keeping us in safety.

If we don't see the connection between shalom and increasing the dominion, kingship, and authority of God, then we're missing out on a lot of scriptural reality. The entire Bible proclaims the shalom of God setting things in order, restoring unity, and bringing harmony between relationships.

RULE ON EARTH THROUGH PEOPLE

When God advances His dominion of peace in the earth, He does it through His people. He longs for us to participate in the establishment of His kingdom, extending His rule and reign of peace. His dominion of peace only increases as it expands in the hearts of individuals. He wants His kingdom of peace to be here on earth just as it is in heaven. That's His method, His Plan A, and there is no Plan B. We are the vehicles to bring that kingdom to bear on planet earth.

Jesus taught us to pray for His kingdom to come and His will to be done on earth as it is in heaven (see Matt. 6:10). He longs to establish His covenant of peace with His people. Victory has to be established within us before we can offer it to others. It has to be real to us—experienced by us.

Peace isn't something we talk about as theoretical. It must be something we experience as a continual lifestyle. The peace must be evident *in* our lives before it will become evident *through* our lives. We cannot give to the world something we don't first experience ourselves. We receive it from heaven and then we're empowered to give it away to others.

God's kingdom of peace comes and reconciles us to Him, to ourselves, and to the world around us. But how does this peace come? Who initiates this realm of peace?

HOLY SPIRIT ENVIRONMENTALISTS

Just as there is an emphasis on natural environmentalism in our day, so God is calling peacemakers in His kingdom to be Holy Spirit environmentalists. What do I mean by this? We should be people who care about the spiritual atmosphere that we're emanating. We can create an atmosphere of peace wherever we go because we are ruled by the dominion of peace. It is impossible to hide our individual atmosphere. We can fool people with our words, we can fool them with our gestures, but we can't hide the atmosphere we emanate.

Every person disperses an atmosphere at all times. Children know the instant a father comes home if he had a bad day at work or if something is bothering him. They can feel it, whether he says a word or not. When I was much younger, I used to hide in the attic when my dad came home for lunch because I knew he emanated a certain pressure. Even if it was 100 degrees outside, I would rather sweat in the attic than be around him. I preferred to be uncomfortable in the attic than spend 45 minutes in his presence, just because I knew he would scold me about something.

We can choose to walk in peace and radiate the presence of peace, or we can choose to walk in anxiety and a lack of trust, emanating a lack of peace. God has given us peace. The question is, "What will we choose?" There are a few different areas affected by kingdom environmentalists.

Affect the World and the Flesh

Kingdom environmentalists will be people who affect the world in which they live. Like Jesus sleeping in the middle of the storm, so we are to be people who change the atmosphere with the words we speak and the presence we emanate. We are not supposed to be conformed to the world, but we are to speak to the storms of life and witness as the peace of God saturates those situations, bringing order out of chaos.

Dennis was once in a meeting in Pennsylvania with Pat Robertson and Ben Kinchlow. They were on the stage when one of them said that everyone needed to pray because a great storm was coming. It was an outdoor event with over 10,000 people present, all of their equipment was exposed, and nothing was protected from the rain. As the storm approached and all the people prayed in unity for a miracle, the blackness split, formed a perfect V, and went around where they were assembled only to reconnect on the other side. They didn't pray out of fear but out of faith. Though this happened in a crowd with many people present, it can also happen on an individual level as well. We are called to affect the world we live in.

Holy Spirit environmentalists are discerning. When Jesus sent out His disciples in Luke 10, He told them that if there was a son of peace there, then they could stay and their peace would rest upon that place. But if there wasn't a son of peace there, then peace would return back to them.

The dove of God's peace is going to rest on lambs, not on wolves. The people I've seen who haven't been able to receive ministry are those who are indifferent, prejudiced, or angry, refusing to forgive. If you've got an anger problem, then deal with it because you're robbing yourself of the good things God has for you.

The whole Book of Ephesians presents a contrast between anger and the grace of God. When we are angry, we forfeit grace. When we live in grace, we are not angry. The only exception is righteous anger, but for the most part the anger of believers is unrighteous. When people are receptive, however, then peace comes and stays. Peace is fruit that remains. James reminds us, *"The anger of man does not achieve the righteousness of God"* (James 1:20 NASB).

Are Identified by Their Fruit

Kingdom people are identified by the fruit they produce. The kingdom of God is demonstrated in righteousness, peace, and joy—fruit that is produced in our lives, not works we do with our own willpower. If we are people on whom the domain of God rests, then we'll produce fruit in accordance with the reign of God.

Jesus said, *"Therefore by their fruits you will know them"* (Matt. 7:20). He doesn't say that we're going to know Christians by their words or by their proper theology. Only the supernatural emotions of God can emanate the fragrance of Christ, and only the love of God can work righteous deeds. The source is everything! A wrong source cannot produce good fruit.

Many believers can talk the talk, but only a small minority actually walk the walk. It seems that everyone talks about love and peace, but few walk in the abundance of them, demonstrating love and peace by their actions. We are called to be people who bear fruit for God's glory. The fruit of peace should permeate *every* area of life, not leaving even one single area outside of His control.

PEACE IS THE WAY

Throughout the Bible peace is described as "the way." I had never paid much attention to that term before, but once we began to study God's shalom intensively throughout the Bible, we saw "the way" in a new light.

John the Baptist was a forerunner of Jesus's ministry. He came before Christ to prepare *the way* for Him to arrive upon the scene. Isaiah 40:3 told of John's ministry, that he would be the voice crying in the wilderness, *"Prepare the way of the Lord; make straight in the desert a highway for our God."* John's very ministry was to prepare the way for the ministry of Jesus, which meant he was to remove obstacles from His path, to bring knowledge of salvation through forgiveness, bring light into darkness, and to reveal the way of peace.

The father of John, the priest Zacharias, doubted the angel Gabriel when the coming birth of John was announced to him. Therefore, the angel told Zacharias he would be unable to speak until the day of fulfillment. When Zacharias, John's father, had his ability to speak restored, he praised God and prophesied, saying:

> *And you, child, will be called the prophet of the Highest; for you will go before the face of the Lord to prepare His ways, to give knowledge of salvation to His people by the remission of their sins, through the tender mercy of our God, with which the Dayspring from on high has visited us; to give light to those who sit in darkness and the shadow of death, to guide our feet into the way of peace* (Luke 1:76-79).

A *way* in life is a course of conduct or manner of living. It includes how we walk step by step and the direction in which we go. Part of the spiritual preparation we need is to have our feet guided "in the way of peace." And part of the purpose of the prophetic voices of our day and hour is to guide the people of God in the way of peace.

Walking in the way of peace guarantees that we're walking in the plans and purposes of God for our lives. Or at least we are walking in the light that we have. When we need more light, God will give it to us. Many Christians pray and then say that they don't know what the will of God is in a specific situation; then they go on with their lives. But the way we discern the will of God is by walking in the way of peace. If you don't know what God's will is, then start moving in what you do know. It is easier for God to work with someone already in motion. If you lose your peace as you move in a particular direction, then it is not the will of God, because His ways are peace.

Peace is a great indicator for married couples when seeking direction for their lives. Your guidance should match. Both of you should have peace about a specific situation before moving ahead in it. If one of you has a green light and the other has a red light, then you should pray and wait until both of your lights match. It is necessary that both agree before moving ahead. Otherwise, you don't yet have the mind of the Lord.

PEACE NEEDS TO BE PREACHED

Because the way of peace is something God is emphasizing now, it is incumbent upon us to preach what He is saying to the church. And when I say it needs to be preached, I don't mean just five-fold preachers and teachers giving sermons from the pulpit. This message of peace needs to be demonstrated and declared through our words and with our actions—by *everyone* in the body of Christ. Let's look at a few Scriptures that connect peace with preaching:

> *The word which God sent to the children of Israel, preaching peace through Jesus Christ* (Acts 10:36).

> *So Jesus said to them again, "Peace to you! As the Father has sent Me, I also send you"* (John 20:21).

And He came and preached peace to you who were afar off and to those who were near (Ephesians 2:17).

How beautiful upon the mountains are the feet of him who brings good news, who proclaims peace, who brings glad tidings of good things, who proclaims salvation, who says to Zion, "Your God reigns!" (Isaiah 52:7)

How then shall they call on Him in whom they have not believed? And how shall they believe in Him of whom they have not heard? And how shall they hear without a preacher? And how shall they preach unless they are sent? As it is written: "How beautiful are the feet of those who preach the gospel of peace, who bring glad tidings of good things!" (Romans 10:14-15)

The power of peace must be proclaimed—peace with God, peace with ourselves, and peace with others. We must live and preach peace with all of our heart. God has given us the fruit of peace, and He has invited us to share in His establishment of peace upon the earth. He longs for us to walk in the way of peace, thus becoming "living epistles." As we engage in a lifestyle of peace, peace won't be a theological concept any longer, but the peace of God will actually *rule* in our hearts (see Col. 3:15).

CHAPTER 7

THE COVENANT OF PEACE

BY DR. JEN

ESTABLISHING HIS COVENANT

The gift of peace, which Jesus gave to us when we were born again, is always available for believers as a fruit of the Spirit. The *covenant of peace* for us today is promised to those who become peacemakers. To receive a covenant of peace requires responsibility on our part.

In the Old Testament, God made a *covenant of peace* with one particular individual, Phinehas, and promised a covenant of peace to His people, Israel (see Num. 25:10-13). A covenant of peace includes all that is contained in the word *shalom*, but it also takes on a far richer meaning.

Contained within the covenant of peace is everything God's children could ever want or need. All of the promises of God are fulfilled in His character and in His nature—there is nothing missing in the covenant of peace. When God truly rules His people and their hearts belong to Him, the blessings of the covenant abound.

In a passage of Scripture reminiscent of the coming millennial kingdom, Ezekiel describes the nature of the covenant of peace. Read carefully what God promised here:

> "I will make a covenant of peace with them, and cause wild beasts to cease from the land; and they will dwell safely in the wilderness and sleep in the woods. I will make them and the places all around My hill a blessing; and I will cause showers to come down in their season; there shall be showers of blessing. Then the trees of the field shall yield their fruit, and the earth shall yield her increase. They shall be safe in their land; and they shall know that I am the Lord, when I have broken the bands of their yoke and delivered them from the hand of those who enslaved them. And they shall no longer be a prey for the nations, nor shall beasts of the land devour them; but they shall dwell safely, and no one shall make them afraid. I will raise up for them a garden of renown, and they shall no longer be consumed with hunger in the land, nor bear the shame of the Gentiles anymore. Thus they shall know that I, the Lord their God, am with them, and

*they, the house of Israel, are My people," says the Lord
God* (Ezekiel 34:25-30).

One of the most profound aspects of this covenant is that it
will never be removed from us. Of course, we can refuse to accept
the covenant of peace, but should we receive it, it will never be
taken away from us because it is an everlasting covenant. God
promises us in Isaiah 54:10, *"For the mountains shall depart and
the hills be removed, but My kindness shall not depart from you,
nor shall My covenant of peace be removed."* His covenant is sure
and His peace only increases.

Moses reminded the Israelites, *"And you shall remember the
Lord your God, for it is He who gives you power to get wealth, that
He may establish His covenant which He swore to your fathers, as
it is this day"* (Deut. 8:18). God wants His covenant established
in the earth, and this only happens through the coming of His
kingdom. When we co-labor with Him for the sake of His kingdom, He will provide everything we need. Jesus said, *"Seek first
the kingdom of God and His righteousness, and all these things will
be added to you"* (Matt. 6:33). God wants us to prosper by establishing His covenant of peace with us.

The purpose for which God gives us wealth is to build His
kingdom on the earth. He does not give us wealth so we can
consume it according to our own lusts (see James 4:3). Unfortunately, even believers often have a tendency to think that we
are smart enough, educated enough, and capable enough to do
many things apart from God. However, our only purpose is to be
yielded vessels through whom God can work to accomplish His

will: *"For it is God who works in you both to will and to do for His good pleasure"* (Phil. 2:13).

We may also lose sight of the fact that we are stewards of God's property. Those who squander God's resources will give an account to Him someday. As His stewards, He expects us to use His resources in a righteous way. Therefore, God has given us the power to get wealth through shalom, because He wants to establish His covenant in the earth. *"The wealth of the sinner is laid up for the righteous,"* the writer of Proverbs reminds us (Prov. 13:22). Those whose mission becomes God's mission will never lack the wealth they need to accomplish God's purposes.

THE COVENANTS OF GOD

A covenant is a binding agreement between two parties. Scripture cites a number of examples of covenants cut between two individuals and also cites others that are between people and God. When *God* establishes a covenant, He is the greater making a pledge with a lesser, because God and humans aren't equal parties. A covenant may or may not be conditional.[1] Three main covenants made by God with humanity include:

- The Old Covenant with Moses

- The New Covenant with Jesus

- The Covenant of Peace with Phinehas see pages 135-138

In the history of humankind, each one of these covenants covers God's dealings with humanity during a particular span of time. The Old Covenant covered the time of the law, the New Covenant was inaugurated through the redemptive work of Jesus Christ on the cross, and we are now on the cusp of the Age of the Kingdom, during which peace will come in fullness. The covenant of peace was first made with Phinehas, a high priest, in Numbers 25:1-13.

OLD COVENANT	NEW COVENANT	AGE OF THE KINGDOM
Covenant of Law	Covenant of Redemption	Covenant of Peace
2000 BC	0–AD 2000	AD 20??-3000

The Old Covenant was initiated by Moses and God and created the *physical nation* of Israel. The New Covenant came through Jesus, at which time God created the *spiritual nation* of the church. These two nations will be brought together by God as "one new man," ushering in an age of peace, or the Age of the Kingdom. Paul writes:

> *For He Himself is our peace, who has made both one, and has broken down the middle wall of separation, having abolished in His flesh the enmity, that is, the law of commandments contained in ordinances, so as to create in Himself one new man from the two, thus making peace, and that He might reconcile them both to God in one body through the cross, thereby putting to death the enmity. And He came and preached peace to you who were afar off and to those who were near* (Ephesians 2:14-17).

The Age of the Kingdom will manifest the shalom of God in all its fullness. The covenant of peace describes the terms of God's peace plan. The kingdom was, is, and is yet to come. What we now see in partial measure will one day be known in full completion.

GOVERNMENT AND PEACE

God's government and peace are inextricably linked together because government brings order and order brings peace. The kingdom of God is a kingdom of shalom, a government of peace, establishing the rule and reign of God wherever it is manifested. Eventually, in the millennial reign of Christ, the kingdom of God will fully come; Babylon, this world's system, will fall, and it will be replaced by God's order of government. Cleansing judgment always precedes blessing.

This same pattern of judgment before blessing is seen throughout Scripture. The Bible names those who share God's zeal for His kingdom "peacemakers" and calls them His sons (see Matt. 5:9). They are those with whom God makes a covenant of peace.

The first coming of Jesus began with His birth. Before His second coming, His fullness will be birthed in His mature sons and daughters, whom the Bible calls the *sons of God*. The Greek word for "child" in the New Testament is *teknon*, both literally and figuratively. It refers to the fact of birth. In our culture today, it is more common to adopt a baby. In the time of Jesus, however, sons were adopted when they reached full maturity, ready to stand shoulder to shoulder with their father and run the family business.

The Greek word used for "son" is *huios* and refers to maturity, dignity, and character—a worthy heir, not a young child. This is what Paul was referencing when he wrote:

> *For as many as are led by the Spirit of God, these are sons of God. For you did not receive the spirit of bondage again to fear, but you received the Spirit of adoption* [mature sonship] *by whom we cry out, "Abba, Father"* (Romans 8:14-15).

MATURE SONSHIP

Just as men are included in the bride of Christ, women are included in the sons of God. The term *bride* refers to intimacy with the Lord, but *son* refers to overcoming conquerors. The "overcomers" in the seven messages to the churches in the Book of Revelation speak of those believers who have attained the status of mature sons of God. They have left childish things behind and now live and work as citizens of heaven—those who *"sit together in the heavenly places in Christ Jesus"* (Eph. 2:6). Paul goes on to say:

> *For I consider that the sufferings of this present time are not worthy to be compared with the glory which shall be revealed in us. For the earnest expectation of the creation eagerly waits for the revealing of the sons of God* (Romans 8:18-19).

The term *son*, then, implies an individual whose only concern is doing the works of Father God, in the same way that Jesus came down from heaven not to do His own will but the will of the Father who sent Him (see John 6:38). We are born again as a *child* of God but we become *sons* of God and heirs only when we become mature in Christ. Paul expands this by saying:

> Now I say that the heir, as long as he is a child, does not differ at all from a slave, though he is master of all, but is under guardians and stewards until the time appointed by the father.... But when the fullness of the time had come, God sent forth His Son, born of a woman, born under the law, to redeem those who were under the law, that we might receive the adoption as sons. And because you are sons, God has sent forth the Spirit of His Son into your hearts, crying out, "Abba, Father!" Therefore you are no longer a slave but a son, and if a son, then an heir of God through Christ (Galatians 4:1-2, 4-7).

For this reason Paul labored in prayer that believers would grow up and "have Christ formed" in them (see Gal. 4:19). T. Austin Sparks says of this:

> God will reach His end; He will come in, in His Son in terms of sonship, to take up residence within those begotten of Him, and will grow in them, increase His measure in them, until at last, brought to the unity of the faith, they become a mighty embodiment and revelation of God Himself. Not in Deity, but in what He is spiritually and morally in this universe—conformed to the image of His Son, a living expression of God's own thoughts.

And the secret? Why, it is just this: "I will go down Myself in terms of sonship and will generate a new race through faith, and that new race will be brought eventually to spiritual full growth; which simply means that then I shall fill all, I shall occupy all the space; there will be no room for anything else at all." That is the issue for every Christian life. It is whether God is going to fill the whole space or not, or whether we are going to have a bit. All the time that is what is going on.[2]

Jesus came to do so much more than get us barely saved. Consider the words, *"For all have sinned and fall short of the glory of God"* (Rom. 3:23). Salvation takes care of our sin problem, but God wants to restore us to the *glory* forfeited by Adam and Eve in the Garden. Jesus offers us a chance to partake of the glory of His kingdom should we choose to accept it. He came to guide us in the way of peace, which ultimately leads us to the glory of His kingdom.

The writer of Hebrews says:

> *For it was fitting for Him, for whom are all things, and through whom are all things, in bringing many sons to glory, to perfect the author of their salvation through sufferings. For both He who sanctifies and those who are sanctified are all from one Father; for which reason He is not ashamed to call them brethren* (Hebrews 2:10-11 NASB).

COVENANT OF PEACE

In the King James Version of the Bible, the word *covenant* is used about 290 times; *peace*, which in Hebrew is *shalom*, is used more than 230 times in the Old Testament; and *peace*, which is the Greek word *eirene*, is used more than 90 times. However, the phrase "covenant of peace" is used directly only four times (although Scripture refers to it indirectly in a number of verses).

The covenant of peace is first mentioned in connection with Phinehas in the Book of Numbers. Just as Abraham is the father of faith, Phinehas could be called the father of peace because he was the first person with whom God established a covenant of peace. God did this because, like Jesus, Phinehas loved righteousness and hated lawlessness (see Ps. 45:6-7; Heb. 1:9). In total, Phinehas was spurred to action in four separate accounts of his righteous acts.

1. The Covenant of Peace with Phinehas

Phinehas, a high priest during the time of the wilderness wanderings, was the grandson of Aaron. At this particular time in Israel's history, the Israelites were committing sexual immorality with the Moabites and Midianites, and, as a result, they were enticed to worship Baal. The Lord was angry and commanded Moses to deal with the offenders. However, Zimri, one of the leaders, instigated a rebellion against Moses.

Immediately, Phinehas rose up in righteous anger and burst into the tent of an Israelite man, catching him in the act with a Midianite woman. He thrust a spear through their bellies, turning away the anger of the Lord and stopping the plague, which had already killed 24,000 people. God commended Phinehas for being zealous with the zeal of the Lord and, as a result, gave him an everlasting covenant of peace (see Num. 25:1-13). His zeal was like that of Jesus in the cleansing of the temple (see Matt. 21:12-14; Luke 19:45-47).

> *Then the Lord spoke to Moses, saying: "Phinehas the son of Eleazar, the son of Aaron the priest, has turned back My wrath from the children of Israel, because he was zealous with My zeal among them, so that I did not consume the children of Israel in My zeal. Therefore say, 'Behold, I give to him My covenant of peace; and it shall be to him and his descendants after him a covenant of an everlasting priesthood, because he was zealous for his God, and made atonement for the children of Israel'"* (Numbers 25:10-13).

Phinehas is mentioned for the second time in Numbers 31:5, when Moses dispatched him to take revenge against the Midianites for harassing and seducing the children of Israel to sin. The third time Phinehas is called to intervene takes place in the Promised Land in Joshua 22, when the Israelites feared that the three tribes who remained in the east side of the Jordan were rebelling against the Lord because they built an altar outside of the tabernacle.

Therefore, Phinehas was sent to confront them. As it turned out, they had merely built an altar as a reminder for their children, not as a place of actual sacrifice. He served as a righteous judge who was not afraid to confront but was careful to avoid hasty judgment. The last situation in which he is mentioned is during a serious conflict between the tribe of Benjamin and the rest of Israel, which became an outright war (see Judges 19–21).

As a militant peacemaker, Phinehas did not fear going into battle. However, he only waged righteous warfare. In all things, Phinehas refused to tolerate unrighteousness but championed justice, like our Prince of Peace, the ultimate peacemaker. To be peacemakers, then, we must also be willing to engage in righteous warfare for the sake of true peace (see 1 John 3:7).

> *For there must also be factions among you, that those who are approved may be recognized among you* (1 Corinthians 11:19).

> *Deliver such a one to Satan for the destruction of the flesh, that his spirit may be saved in the day of the Lord Jesus* (1 Corinthians 5:5).

> *For we do not wrestle against flesh and blood, but against principalities, against powers, against the rulers of the darkness of this age, against spiritual hosts of wickedness in the heavenly places* (Ephesians 6:12).

2. The Covenant of Peace in Isaiah

In Isaiah 54, God speaks words of comfort to a grieving, barren woman, who is a type of the bride of Christ. She is first chastised because of sin but then blessed with a covenant of peace and a promise for her children, the spiritual offspring of Phinehas:

> *"For this is like the waters of Noah to Me; for as I have sworn that the waters of Noah would no longer cover the earth, so have I sworn that I would not be angry with you, nor rebuke you. For the mountains*

shall depart and the hills be removed, but My kind-
ness shall not depart from you, nor shall My covenant
of peace be removed," says the Lord, who has mercy on
you.... "All your children shall be taught by the Lord,
and great shall be the peace of your children" (Isaiah
54:9-10, 13).

3. The Covenant of Peace: Judgment against God's Shepherds in Ezekiel 34

God judges the unrighteous shepherds but promises to bless
His people with a covenant of peace.

And the word of the Lord came to me, saying, "Son of
man, prophesy against the shepherds of Israel, proph-
esy and say to them, 'Thus says the Lord God to the
shepherds: "Woe to the shepherds of Israel who feed
themselves! Should not the shepherds feed the flocks?
You eat the fat and clothe yourselves with the wool; you
slaughter the fatlings, but you do not feed the flock.
The weak you have not strengthened, nor have you
healed those who were sick, nor bound up the broken,
nor brought back what was driven away, nor sought
what was lost; but with force and cruelty you have
ruled them. So they were scattered because there was
no shepherd; and they became food for all the beasts of
the field when they were scattered. My sheep wandered
through all the mountains, and on every high hill;
yes, My flock was scattered over the whole face of the
earth, and no one was seeking or searching for them"'"
(Ezekiel 34:1-6).

4. The Covenant of Peace: Blessing of Israel in Ezekiel 37

Ezekiel 37 describes two visions pertaining to the restoration of Israel. The first vision describes the valley of dry bones that comes to life and becomes a great army. The second vision was of two sticks, one representing Judah (natural Israel) and the other spiritual Israel (the church) (see Ezek. 37:15-23). They become one in the hand of the Lord under a covenant of peace.

> *Then they shall be My people, and I will be their God.... Moreover I will make a covenant of peace with them, and it shall be an everlasting covenant with them; I will establish them and multiply them, and I will set My sanctuary in their midst forevermore. My tabernacle also shall be with them; indeed I will be their God, and they shall be My people. The nations also will know that I, the Lord, sanctify Israel, when My sanctuary is in their midst forevermore* (Ezekiel 37:23,26-28).

THE KINGDOM AGE

Eventually, the millennial reign of Christ will be ushered in, first with judgment for cleansing, and then the blessings of the covenant of peace will be released in fullness. This is where God's kingdom of peace is fully established, reversing the effects of the fall, restoring perfect shalom in every area of life:

> *He shall judge between the nations, and rebuke many people; they shall beat their swords into plowshares, and their spears into pruning hooks; nation shall not*

lift up sword against nation, neither shall they learn war anymore (Isaiah 2:4).

And again:

The wolf also shall dwell with the lamb, the leopard shall lie down with the young goat, the calf and the young lion and the fatling together; and a little child shall lead them. The cow and the bear shall graze; their young ones shall lie down together; and the lion shall eat straw like the ox. The nursing child shall play by the cobra's hole, and the weaned child shall put his hand in the viper's den. They shall not hurt nor destroy in all My holy mountain, for the earth shall be full of the knowledge of the Lord as the waters cover the sea (Isaiah 11:6-9).

ENDNOTES

1. P. Jablonowski, *Sons to Glory* (Harvest, AL: Free eBook, 2006), 37-63. Accessed on November 12, 2012, from http://sonstoglory.com/book.htm.

2. T. A. Sparks, "The Need for a New Apprehension of the Gospel," The Online Library of T. Austin Sparks. (An extract from *The Fight of the Faith*, Chapter 5. First published in A Witness and A Testimony magazine, May-June 1943, Vol. 21-3). Accessed on July 12, 2013, from http://www.austin-sparks.net/english/000525.html.

CHAPTER 8

POWER PEACE IS
WARFARE PEACE

By Dennis

PEACE PROVIDES SAFETY
AND SECURITY

Jesus is the Prince of Peace and *"He Himself is our peace"* (Eph. 2:14). Peace is life changing. Peace is powerful. When His peace guards our heart and mind, we are safe because no foe can get past Him (see Phil. 4:7). In Him, we are safe and secure. However, we are not only safe, we are victorious because the God of peace crushes the enemy beneath our feet (see Rom. 16:20). Jesus has *"given you authority over all the power of the enemy, and you can walk among snakes and scorpions and crush them. Nothing will injure you"* (Luke 10:19 NLT).

As we rest in God's shalom, He promises to keep us in perfect peace—*shalom shalom*. The doubling of a word is a Hebrew method of expressing emphasis. Isaiah said, *"You will keep him in perfect peace, whose mind is stayed on You, because he trusts in You"* (Isa. 26:3). The word *mind* in this verse is not the usual Hebrew word. This particular word, *yêtser*, does not refer to mental reasoning but rather to creative imagination, the seat of plans and ideas. When our trust is in the Lord, we are at peace. And when we have peace, we are open to revelation from God so we are not left to our own resources. He not only protects us but gives us warfare strategy.

With the shalom of God we are able to overcome whatever circumstances we may face. Jesus said, *"I have told you these things, so that in Me you may have [perfect] peace and confidence. In the world you have tribulation and trials and distress and frustration; but be of good cheer [take courage; be confident, certain, undaunted]! For I have overcome the world. [I have deprived it of power to harm you and have conquered it for you]"* (John 16:33 AMP). Everyone has trials in life, but we cannot be harmed when peace guards us. Moreover, God will take whatever the enemy meant for destruction, turn it around, and use it for our good.

POWER PEACE IS MILITANT

The world thinks personal peace consists of happy thoughts and pleasant circumstances. However, the peace of Jesus is power—a supernatural peace that's unconquerable. Peace isn't passive. Peace is militant. It establishes dominion wherever it is manifested.

The peace of God is impenetrable spiritual armor. The peace of God will *"guard your hearts and minds through Christ Jesus"*

(Phil. 4:7). We are instructed to wear *shoes of peace* in order to stand firm against the onslaughts of the enemy and walk confidently in the power of peace (see Eph. 6:15).

In the example found in the introduction of this book, peace guarded me and empowered me to stand without wavering when confronted by a desperate, knife-wielding inmate in a halfway house. The armor of peace really did guard my heart and mind as well as keep me physically safe. Remember, however, that we should stand when God tells us to stand but go when God tells us to go. David constantly inquired to know God's strategy for each particular situation he found himself in. Relationship asks questions; religion makes rules.

At another time, Jen and I left a retail store in a strip mall. We exited on the side of a large building that extended far back toward a wooded area. Suddenly, a man appeared out of the woods quite a distance away. I felt an evil presence but did not lose my peace. I could feel the ominous presence outside of me, but I was also aware of peace in my heart. That is discerning of spirits. When you have peace inside, you can sense the outside atmosphere without giving in to it. The Lord spoke to me, "Get in your car now!"

I told Jen to get in the car and not to ask questions. We were only five or six feet away from our car and immediately flung open the doors, hopped in, and locked the doors. It felt like a power shield of peace was surrounding our car. But as soon as we got in and locked the doors, he was at my car window. It was as though a dark force had supernaturally translated him. We quickly drove away, never once losing our peace.

Sometimes the Lord will direct us to stand our ground. At other times, He will prompt us to take quick action. If I had given in to fear, it could have blocked me from hearing God and acting so quickly. All the peace Scriptures are not mere platitudes or clever sayings. They are meant to be applied in everyday life.

God is the author of peace. No supernatural peace is manifested apart from Him. His kingdom of peace is always on the increase, always expanding, and always establishing dominion. Peace isn't passive.

God's government of peace is like a military coup. The conquering King of Peace enters triumphantly, displaces the enemy, and establishes His rule in the earth. The victory has been won. We simply enter into what He has already accomplished. It is time for the church to shake off passivity and enter into aggressive Christianity and the warfare of peace.

The supernatural power peace that wields has tremendous authority. It takes dominion and brings its rule to bear wherever it manifests. Peace is kingly, authoritative, and it governs. Romans 5:17 in the Amplified Bible says that believers can *reign as kings in life* because of God's overflowing grace. We must diligently pursue peace because this is the time for the army of the Lord to come forth.

Not long ago, I had a vision of Jesus rising up as a mighty warrior with the sweat of battle on His brow and a shout of victory in His mouth. As He arose, He broke through a net made from the slimy strands of interconnecting human agendas and unclean soul ties and defeated the schemes of the enemy to keep the church entrapped in the things of the world. *"The Lord shall go forth like a mighty man; He shall stir up His zeal like a man of war. He shall cry out, yes, shout aloud; He shall prevail against His enemies"* (Isa. 42:13).

When we have no peace, the kingdom of evil can operate freely, creating chaos, disturbance, and anarchy. In peace, we are unconquerable because we are in Christ.

THE POWER OF DISPLACEMENT

Power peace operates by a basic principle of spiritual warfare—the power of *displacement*. Light and darkness cannot coexist. As soon as the light comes on, darkness flees. When God comes in, demons automatically take flight. When God sets up residence in an area of our heart, the enemy is cast out.

Negative emotions cannot exist in God's kingdom. They are the product of the kingdom of darkness. If God didn't give them, why should we allow them to remain in our heart? When God heals wounds in the heart, He takes that territory back from the enemy. When God comes in, He exchanges negative emotions for the fruit of the Spirit. The territory occupied by peace in our heart expands.

If the power of displacement claims territory for God in individual hearts, the power of displacement can also bring entire cities and nations under the government of God. When revival breaks out in the land, principalities and powers are displaced by the presence of God.

When a demon is cast out of a person, it roams around, seeking to gather more demons so it can try and return. If that space has been occupied, the demon has no place to return. However, if it finds the space clean and put in order, then it will come back much more powerful than when it left (see Matt. 12:43-45).

We don't kill demons—they don't cease to exist after we cast them out. We don't stab them and then watch them bleed and die. When we defeat a demon, we serve notice that God's shalom now resides in the space it previously populated. The peace of God now rules in that area that was previously occupied by the enemy. The peace of God displaces evil. Where demons used to have access, they no longer have access because God is there.

In spiritual warfare peace displaces the chaos, the lack, and the anarchy first within us and then it is brought to bear on those things outside of us. If we want the government of God's peace to win the battle outside of us, then we must yield to His peace within. When we have peace in our heart, we have the power to resist evil influences outside of us. When we yield to peace and resist the enemy, the peace of God's presence surrounds us and pushes back the forces of darkness. God's kingdom of peace is, therefore, established by the power of displacement.

GIDEON AND POWER PEACE

The story of Gideon demonstrates the warfare of peace we are speaking about. The Book of Judges tells of a time when the children of Israel had sinned against the Lord, so He delivered them into the hand of the Midianites for seven years. The Israelites hid in caves and mountain strongholds while the Midianite armies ravaged the land and impoverished Israel.

In the midst of all the destruction, Gideon was threshing wheat in the wine press, hiding in fear of the Midianites (wheat would normally have been threshed out in the open). Suddenly, the Lord appeared and said to him, *"The Lord is with you, you mighty man of valor!"* (Judg. 6:12).

Gideon answered, "Who, me?" He began to make excuses to God about why he was *not* qualified to be a warrior. "O my Lord, how can I save Israel? Indeed my clan is the weakest in Manasseh, and I am the least in my father's house," said Gideon. Then he asks, "Where are all the miracles now that God did long ago?" Judging from this response, he certainly doesn't seem like a mighty man of valor.

> *Now Gideon perceived that He was the Angel* (messenger) *of the Lord. So Gideon said, "Alas, O Lord God! For I have seen the Angel* (messenger) *of the Lord face to face." Then the Lord said to him, "Peace be with you; do not fear, you shall not die." So Gideon built an altar there to the Lord, and called it The-Lord-Is-Peace* (Jehovah-Shalom) *(Judges 6:22-24).*[1]

The law of first mention is the principle of studying the portion of the Scriptures where a name or principle is first cited in the Bible. The name of God, Jehovah-Shalom, or "The Lord is Peace," is introduced in the story of Gideon. This manifestation of the Lord changed him from a man of fear into a man of peace. Now that Gideon was a man of peace, he could be used as God's man of war.

The Lord explained that Gideon was going to save Israel from the hand of the Midianites because God had sent him. And then the Lord promises, *"Surely I will be with you, and you shall defeat the Midianites as one man"* (Judg. 6:16). God raised up

Gideon to be a leader of an army of 300 men, but they defeated the Midianites as "one man." Unity will be a vital strategy for the church in the coming days.

Unity is not a doctrinal concept, project unity, or mere congeniality. True unity requires real relationship. In the upper room, the disciples came into one accord, or "one heart." In the case of a Gideon's army, soldiers became a band of brothers.

> *I, therefore, the prisoner of the Lord, beseech you to walk worthy of the calling with which you were called, with all lowliness and gentleness, with longsuffering, bearing with one another in love, endeavoring to keep the unity of the Spirit in the bond of peace* (Ephesians 4:1-3).

The word "bond" here is *sundesmos* in the Greek, meaning "that which binds together." It is the same word as ligaments that hold bones together as well as heart knittings that unite the church. Bones may be many and varied, but they are useless if they are disconnected. Ligaments connect the bones to one another, allowing the body to move and function as a single entity, a living organism.

"One new man" is a corporate expression of the church. As we come together in unity, we open a portal that releases the kingdom of heaven on earth. The psalmist wrote, *"Behold, how good and how pleasant it is for brethren to dwell together in unity! It is like the precious oil upon the head, running down on the beard, the beard of Aaron, running down on the edge of his garments"* (Ps. 133:1-2).

This is Jesus's prayer for us as well (see John 17:21).[2] Peace empowers us to walk in the abundant life God has for us, including satisfying, healthy relationships. The binding power of peace knits us together in relational ways we never dreamed possible. We begin to know one another by the spirit rather than fleshly personality (see 2 Cor. 5:16), and the bonds of peace can draw us together as one man.

GOD SPEAKS TO POTENTIAL

Gideon responded to the Lord by saying, *"If now I have found favor in Your sight, then show me a sign that it is You who talk with me. Do not depart from here, I pray, until I come to You and bring out my offering and set it before You"* (Judg. 6:17-18). Gideon was working on his fear and insecurity here.

God always speaks to our potential, not to what we are now. God called him a mighty man of valor, but Gideon reacted like many of us do today: "Oh, yeah, right. How come I can't do this? How come I can't do that? Why doesn't this happen when I pray? I'm not a mighty man of God." But God is very patient and He works with us. He wants to establish His dominion of peace within us, which causes fear and insecurity to evaporate.

God not only released Gideon's hidden potential but He also stirred up militancy in him. Gideon prepared a young goat and some unleavened bread and presented them to the Lord. God instructed him to put the items on the rock, and he did so. Then the Lord stretched out the end of his staff, touched the rock, and fire came up out of the rock and consumed the meat and unleavened bread. Gideon knew that something big was going on.

Now Gideon perceived that He was the Angel of the Lord. So Gideon said, "Alas, O Lord God! For I have

> *seen the Angel of the Lord face to face." Then the Lord said to him, "Peace be with you; do not fear, you shall not die." So Gideon built an altar there to the Lord, and called it The-Lord-Is-Peace* (Judges 6:22-24).

As a result of this experience with God as Jehovah-Shalom, Gideon became a new man. He then had to walk out the revelation of the God of peace in real life. Most of us are good at getting revelation from God but not so adept at walking out what God has revealed to us. We can know revelation as information alone or allow it to produce true transformation within us. We shouldn't go from one revelation to the next, without allowing the revelation to change us. God revealed Himself to Gideon, but Gideon had to *live* the revelation. Peace is powerful. Peace is militant. Peace must be lived.

However, the Lord deals with us one step at a time. When the Lord appeared to Gideon, He said:

> *Take your father's young bull, the second bull of seven years old, and tear down the altar of Baal that your father has, and cut down the wooden image that is beside it; and build an altar to the Lord your God on top of this rock in the proper arrangement, and take the second bull and offer a burnt sacrifice with the wood of the image which you shall cut down* (Judges 6:25-26).

To his credit, Gideon obeyed what God spoke to him even though he was still in the *process* of overcoming his fear. Instead of tearing down the altars during the day, he decided to do it at night. God revealed Himself to Gideon, but Gideon had to take incremental steps before his inner transformation was complete. The good news is that God only requires us to take one step of obedience at a time. Baby steps of obedience build spiritual strength. When the appointed time came, Gideon was prepared to be a mighty man of valor.

TESTED BY THE WATER

Before Gideon and the Israelites could be used to defeat the Midianites, there had to be some testing that took place. Thirty-two thousand men volunteered to go to the battle against them, but God knew that was too many. He didn't want Israel to be able to say that their own hand had saved them. God wanted to make sure Israel couldn't give themselves any credit for the coming victory.

God instructed Gideon to tell those who were fearful or timid to go home. Twenty-two thousand men went home and 10,000 remained. That was still too many. God then instructed Gideon to bring them down to a nearby stream so He could test them there. As the men drank from the stream, the majority lay down flat to drink right out of the stream, but 300 cupped the water in their hands to drink. God said to accept the 300 who drank from their hands. God said, *"By the three hundred men who lapped I will save you, and deliver the Midianites into your hand. Let all the other people go, every man to his place"* (Judg. 7:7).

God then sent Gideon on a stealth mission, and told him to creep into the Midianite camp in the middle of the night. While there, Gideon overheard a man telling his tent mate about a nightmare he had in which a loaf of barley rolled into the camp and defeated them. The man to whom he was telling the dream said it must refer to Gideon.

> *And when Gideon had come, there was a man telling a dream to his companion. He said, "I have had a dream: to my surprise, a loaf of barley bread tumbled into the camp of Midian; it came to a tent and struck it so that it fell and overturned, and the tent collapsed." Then his companion answered and said, "This is nothing else but the sword of Gideon the son of Joash, a man of Israel! Into his hand God has delivered Midian and the whole camp"* (Judges 7:13-14).

The Lord assured Gideon, *"Surely I will be with you, and you shall defeat the Midianites as one man"* (Judg. 6:16). "One loaf of barley bread" was the strategy of unity. Gideon worshiped and then returned to the camp to encourage his men. The army of 300 would win as *one man*. God allowed Gideon to receive a little bit of confirmation about God's plans.

Next, Gideon shared God's strategy with his army. He divided his army of 300 into three companies. *"He put a trumpet into every man's hand, with empty pitchers, and torches inside the pitchers"* (Judg. 7:16). These 300 men were not only fearless and unified, but they had the capacity to work together, to follow instructions, and to respect leadership. I don't know about you, but being handed a torch and clay pitcher on my way to battle wouldn't make me feel well armed. However, when God gives a strategy, logic doesn't count—obedience does. When Gideon blew the trumpet, the 300 men were told to break their pitchers and shout, *"The sword of the Lord and of Gideon!"* (Judg. 7:20).

This demonstrates tremendous God-confidence. The 300 stood with courage despite the odds. They were rooted in the peace of God, knowing they were going to prevail against the Midianites because God had already made them victorious.

> *And every man stood in his place all around the camp; and the whole army ran and cried out and fled. When the three hundred blew the trumpets, the Lord set every man's sword against his companion throughout the whole camp; and the army fled to Beth Acacia, toward Zererah, as far as the border of Abel Meholah, by Tabbath* (Judges 7:21-22).

DIVIDED SPOILS

When we walk in the peace of God, the enemy is perplexed. Peace brings confusion into the enemy's camp. When we walk in the peace of God, the light of God manifests in the earth and blinds the enemy. Darkness can't understand, extinguish, or overcome the light (see John 1:5). We can confound and overcome the enemy because shalom is militant and powerful.

> *Through the tender mercy of our God, with which the Dayspring from on high has visited us; to give light to those who sit in darkness and the shadow of death, to guide our feet into the way of peace* (Luke 1:78-79).

God didn't send an elite team of special ops to defeat the Midianites. He sent an army without weapons. Peace and unity are better than swords and spears. The 300 didn't keep all the spoils of the victory for themselves. They didn't have a private celebration and exclude the cowardly and those who failed to drink water properly. Gideon included all Israel in sharing the spoils—they shared everything. When God's army wins the battle, no one is excluded. Everyone shares in the bounty that comes with success.

The story of Gideon shows us that God can take our fears, insecurities, and weaknesses and change who we are. Christ is the answer for everything we need to accomplish great things in God. He exchanges our deficiencies for His sufficiency. When we know the Lord as Jehovah-Shalom, He can transform the weakest of us into mighty warriors. We can be more than conquerors because of the Lord.

THREE AREAS FOR REFORMATION

To walk in supernatural power peace, we must learn three lessons from the life of Gideon. First, we must be God-focused instead of self-focused. Our whole society is consumed with self—self-esteem, self-actualization, self-improvement, and self-absorption.

Gideon's focus shifted from himself and his apparent disqualifications to the Lord. When we become God-focused, we live in a constant awareness of God and maintain a spiritual connection with Him—practicing the presence of God. Christ in you, your hope of glory, is with you (see Col. 1:27).

Many believers, unfortunately, have the tendency to relate primarily to God as though He is far away in heaven. Distance is a deception. The truth is that Christ dwells within us and His supernatural peace springs up from within. However, when we begin to focus on "God with us," Immanuel, we begin to walk in a greater measure of God's peace and abundant blessings (see Matt. 1:23).

The second lesson we must learn is to be God-searched rather than self-searched. Gideon had no idea of the potential hidden inside him, but God did. The Lord also understood exactly what Gideon needed to be set free. Every time Gideon asked God a question, the Lord answered. The only thing required of Gideon was to keep his focus on God and be obedient. That is how we should live—always trusting, always inquiring, and always obedient.

Psalm 139:23-24 says, *"Search me, O God, and know my heart; try me, and know my anxieties; and see if there is any wicked way in me, and lead me in the way everlasting."* David admitted that he didn't know what was in his own heart, so he asked God to do the searching for him. In Psalms 19:12, David cried out to the Lord, *"How can I know all the sins lurking in my heart? Cleanse me from these hidden faults"* (NLT).

We need the same humility Gideon and David had. Only God knows the entirety of our heart. Self-analysis and intro-spection are a waste of time compared to the knowledge and wisdom of God. Most Christian counseling models combine counselor searching and us searching ourselves. However, when God searches us, He knows exactly where the "knots" are as well as how to untangle them. The Lord knows the perfect timing and proper sequence. He gives us grace to deal with whatever He shows to us.

Third, we need to learn to be God-protected, not self-protected. Gideon was not only incapable of personally protecting himself, but his whole nation was overrun by an army. On his own, Gideon's only strategy was to hide in fear. When we are self-focused and self-searched, we automatically try to protect ourselves. If we don't trust God to protect us, what recourse do we have in the flesh? We resort to carnal weapons. We fight control with control, we run away, or we hide by putting up a wall. That wall is a wall of flesh, and is a product of our *will*.

> *For though we walk in the flesh, we do not war according to the flesh. For the weapons of our warfare are not carnal but mighty in God for pulling down strongholds* (2 Corinthians 10:3-4).

The most unfortunate thing about putting up a wall is that it doesn't work. It is a "fear wall" and the enemy can go right through it. Have you ever had someone say unkind things to you while you had your wall up? Did it stop the words from hurting you? Of course not.

Let God protect you by dropping down into His presence in you and tapping in to the supernatural peace in your heart. Jesus gave it to you as a gift. Try it. It works. It may seem unnatural at first because you have become accustomed to putting up walls, but the Scriptures say God's peace will be your guard: *"The peace of God, which surpasses all understanding, will guard your hearts and minds through Christ Jesus"* (Phil. 4:7).

Now, mind you, we are not telling you to open your heart to a hostile person. We are encouraging you to open your heart to *God*. When you open to God, *He* will stand between you and anything the world can throw at you. The enemy can't touch the fruit of the Spirit. Jesus Himself is our peace, and for anything to touch us, it has to get past *Him*—but we have to actively tap into peace to benefit from His protection.

How did things work out for Gideon when he trusted in the Lord's protection? Wonderfully well for both himself and the whole nation of Israel. Although we may not be in a war with the Midianites, we must learn that God will protect us when we turn to Him. The Lord has given us the refuge of peace within and He knows the strategies to win the battles without.

FULL OF POWER

God's peace is supernatural and it is full of power. As we experience the Prince of Peace more and more and as we live out of the shalom of God, we will see His kingdom of peace reign victorious in our lives. We are called to live in the supernatural power of peace as mighty men and women of valor.

PRACTICE

Spiritual Warfare

Many Christians say they are in spiritual warfare on a regular basis, but the enemy cannot harass us unless he has permission to do so. How do we give him permission to torment us?

Negative Emotions

We give the enemy permission when we fail to deal with negative emotions. Any negative emotion in our heart indicates a need for forgiveness. Our own unforgiveness invites torment.

To bring the warfare to an end, take back the ground given to the enemy by forgiving (see Matt. 18:21-35). All we have to do is close our eyes in prayer and let the Lord show us where we gave the devil a foothold. Picture the first person or situation that comes to mind. Feel the unpleasant emotion and let Christ the forgiver within go to it and through it. As soon as the toxic emotion is washed out, we have peace. When we have peace, we are victorious.

Soulish Prayers (Controlling Prayers)

Occasionally, believers get a headache that feels like a band that goes completely around the head or suddenly a sense of confusion. If you believe this is the case, try forgiveness. Allow a river of forgiveness to flow out from Christ within toward the person(s) who is speaking or praying contrary to the will of God in your life. (You don't have to know who is responsible.) Next, receive forgiveness from Christ in you for anything you may have opened up to accidently.

ENDNOTE

1. The Lord appeared to Gideon in a theophany, or manifestation of God to man. Although the word angel is used in the text, it literally means messenger. Most Bible scholars concur that the Lord appeared to Gideon, not an actual angelic being. It was appropriate for Gideon to present an offering to God but not to an angel.

2. A group of persecuted believers sought refuge on the estate of Count Nicolaus Von Zinzendorf. They did not seek "community" for its own sake. They sought God corporately, were knit together by God into unity, and

on August 13, 1727, experienced an outpouring of revival that is now called the Moravian Pentecost. It initiated a prayer movement that continued around the clock for 100 years and launched radical, fearless missionaries around the globe. Many years later, on his deathbed, Von Zinzendorf said that he had seen Jesus's prayer for unity in John 17 answered in his lifetime.

A Moravian historian wrote that church history abounds in records of "special outpourings of the Holy Ghost, and verily the thirteenth of August 1727, was a day of the outpouring of the Holy Spirit. We saw the hand of God and His wonders, and we were all under the cloud of our fathers baptized with their Spirit. The Holy Ghost came upon us and in those days great signs and wonders took place in our midst. From that time scarcely a day passed but what we beheld His almighty workings amongst us.... Everyone desired above everything else that the Holy Spirit might have full control. Self love and self will, as well as all disobedience, disappeared and an overwhelming flood of graces swept us all out into the great ocean of Divine Love. [J. Greenfield's "Power from on High." Edinburgh: Marshall, Morgan and Scott.© Renewal Journal #1 (93:1), Brisbane, Australia, 2432. Accessed on October 30, 2012, from http://www.pastornet.net.au/renewal/.]

Part III

THE POWER OF PEACE

CHAPTER 9

THE CENTRALITY OF PEACE

BY DENNIS

THE POWER OF PEACE

True spiritual maturity is not determined by our knowledge of biblical information or by knowing about God. Spiritual maturity depends upon a number of variables including consecration, diligence, and intimacy with God. However, spiritual maturity cannot progress beyond our *emotional* maturity. I'm not referring to carnal emotions, of course. Some people can be emotionally well-balanced without being born again. However, a believer cannot be more spiritually mature than their emotions permit. Emotional baggage short-circuits our growth and sabotages our gifts. When we deal with our negative emotions, however, the fruit of the Spirit accelerates our spiritual growth.

The degree to which we walk in the peace of God determines the level of our spiritual influence and depth of maturity. Peace is a necessary prerequisite for all we do in the kingdom of God. If the source is not peace, the result is not acceptable to God. Anything other than the fruit of the Spirit is not life giving. We simply waste our time doing dead works.

Emotional wounding stunts emotional growth. When we remove an emotional barrier through forgiveness, we can grow spiritually. Forgiveness is instant. Maturity requires a process over a period of time, but when we remove blockages we can grow very quickly in the Spirit, in much the same way time-lapse photography shows the accelerated growth of a plant.

One of the missing ingredients in the church today is the reality of peace in the lives of believers. Only the fruit of the Spirit makes everything flow together under the authority of God. Tommy Tenney, author of *The God Chasers*, tells the story of a very large man who stopped by the house of his friend. He stood at the threshold of the front door and looked around the room. No chair was strong enough to hold his weight, so he turned and left. Many visitations of God have come and gone, but God wants a dwelling place (see Eph. 2:22). He is looking for a "chair" so He can stay.

Before God comes to rest in our midst, He must prepare for Himself a place to dwell. The apostolic anointing is designed to bring unity in the body of Christ so God's glory can be manifested in our assemblies. We will never be able to have true unity until we have peace in our hearts, one accord in our relationships, and the God of Peace in our midst.

Peace is not meant to be experienced just on an individual level but on a corporate one—it is necessary for true unity. Unless we come together in unity, we cannot expect outpourings of the Spirit like on the day of Pentecost. Unity creates a portal through which God's glory can come to rest upon us as He promised.

A few years ago, Jen saw of vision of multitudes of small "upper rooms" forming all over the earth. As the believers came into one accord, she heard a great sound like the waters of Niagara Falls, and the glory of God exploded in gatherings of believers around the world. As she looked down upon the earth from a heavenly vantage point, the glory spilled out of the meetings onto the streets, into cities and nations, covering land and sea, and became brighter and brighter. The entire globe began to glow with radiant, golden light. Truly the whole earth was *"filled with the knowledge of the glory of the Lord, as the waters cover the sea"* (Hab. 2:14). If God's glory is going to cover the earth like the waters cover the sea, we must be people who become one with God and one another and align with what God is doing in the earth.

The revelation of the God of Peace is going to be a pivotal message for the body of Christ in the days ahead. It will mark the beginning of a new season and a new movement of God. A revival brings repentance and refreshing to the church. But a movement changes the way church is done.

The army of the Lord will soon arise as the God of Peace rules His church: *"The Lord shall go forth like a mighty man; He shall stir up His zeal like a man of war. He shall cry out, yes, shout aloud; He shall prevail against His enemies"* (Isa. 42:13). For the church to rise up as the army of the Lord, we must be aligned under the authority of our Commander and unified with one another.

Our flesh is vulnerable, but the enemy can't touch the fruit of the Spirit. Nothing—neither flesh nor demonic spirits—can penetrate peace, because Jesus Himself is our peace (see Eph. 2:14). The *"peace of God, which surpasses all understanding, will guard your hearts and minds through Christ Jesus"* (Phil. 4:7). God advances the rule of His kingdom through peace (see Isa. 9:6-7). The God of Peace is militant, and only peace can *"crush Satan beneath our feet"* (Rom. 16:20). Peace is armor. Unless we wear *"shoes of peace,"* how can we walk in our authority in Christ (see Eph. 6:15)?

PEACE IS PRACTICAL

Peace is extremely practical as well. You can't put armor on wounded soldiers. The Lord, therefore, promises the wounded body of Christ that He will heal us and reveal to us *"the abundance of peace and truth"* (Jer. 33:6). When our heart is healed, we experience the supernatural power of peace. When we are connected to peace, we flow in the will of God. Everywhere God's will is done, the kingdom of God triumphs over the kingdom of darkness.

As soon as we drop down and yield to God's will, we experience peace in our heart. God's presence and His peace are available to us at all times, no matter where we are or in what situation we may find ourselves. We don't have to be in the prayer closet to drop down and sense peace. We should enjoy it when we're at work, on our commute home, or even when our computer crashes. Because of the power of peace, the riches of the kingdom of God are continually at hand. The peace of God is our ticket into the abundant life!

God's peace is the peace that *"surpasses all understanding"* (Phil. 4:7), meaning it is far superior to our thoughts, choices, and emotions. The Greek work for "surpass" is *huperballō*, which means "to exceed, go beyond the limits, transcend, or excel." God's supernatural peace is supremely better, higher, and more excellent than anything that comes from our human thinking, choosing, or feeling. Jesus said, *"Peace I leave with you; My peace I give you. I do not give to you as the world gives. Do not let your hearts be troubled and do not be afraid"* (John 14:27 NIV).

When we yield to Christ, we open our heart, yield our will, and surrender ourselves into His arms of love, trusting that God is faithful to care for us, no matter what circumstances we may face. Yielding is a place of total trust and rest—loving assurance that God is in control. When we relax our will and yield to Christ, we let go of any need to control people or situations, and we enter into a lifestyle of radical trust.

THE FIVE Gs OF PEACE

To more completely comprehend the scope of peace, it is helpful to understand five aspects of God's peace, all beginning with the letter *G*. The peace of God works in five arenas of life. When Jesus ascended on high, He Himself divided and gave His mantle for church building to five-fold ministers—His gifts to the church (see Eph. 4:11-16).

Each of these Gs first relates to the five-fold ministry of the apostle, prophet, evangelist, pastor, and teacher. They are given as gifts from Jesus Christ to the body of Christ to equip and mature the saints. Peace must have its work within us if we are to grow up into all that God has for us.

For churches to function under the full mantle of Christ, five-fold ministers must operate as teams. In this context, the apostle is like the architect and general overseer on a construction site who governs the work being done. Apostles are pioneers and church planters. The prophet guides through hearing and proclaiming the "now" word of the Lord. *"The testimony of Jesus is the spirit of prophecy"* (Rev. 19:10). The prophet stirs up vision within the congregation so they can see into God's plans for the future. *"Where there is no vision [no redemptive revelation of God], the people perish"* (Prov. 29:18 AMP). The evangelist reaches out to the lost for soul winning and discipleship, gathering the lost and bringing them into a congregation of believers for healing and equipping. Through discipleship, the saved are equipped to gather together for unity. The pastor cares for the flock and guards them. The teacher teaches and grounds the congregation in the foundational doctrines and truth of the Word of God as well as the practical application of biblical principles.

However, all aspects of five-fold ministry are contained within the shalom commanded by the Prince of Peace. Only supernatural peace can bring order into chaos and expand the kingdom of God on earth. Jesus establishes His government, or rule, on earth and in our life through peace. Jesus governs and establishes the kingdom of God through shalom; therefore, it is quite appropriate for us to think of the mantle of Christ in terms of the five Gs of peace.

Govern

The first aspect of peace is that it governs. Where peace rules, Jesus is ruling. When Jesus governs, everything is rightly established and aligned with Him. When the peace of God governs us, we learn to walk in such a way that it rules our hearts and our minds. Paul wrote to the Colossians, exhorting them to let the peace of God govern their hearts. The Amplified Bible says it this way:

> *And let the peace (soul harmony which comes) from Christ rule (act as umpire continually) in your hearts [deciding and settling with finality all questions that arise in your minds, in that peaceful state] to which as [members of Christ's] one body you were also called [to live]. And be thankful (appreciative), [giving praise to God always]* (Colossians 3:15 AMP).

To *umpire* means that we get out of the way and let Jesus be Lord. He gets to make all the decisions at all times. When the peace of God governs us, we let God be the final authority on all matters related to life. His peace dictates when we move forward or when we move back or whether or not we move at all. His peace continually acts as an umpire in every decision we make and every step that we take. We become obedient even when we don't understand or would prefer our own way.

When believers insist on what they want regardless of God's will in the matter, they are operating in lust. In their day-to-day routine, if Christians would just apply this principle of allowing God to rule within, they would walk in the will of God because peace would be ruling their hearts. When Jesus truly is our King, we will allow Him to govern our heart by His peace.

Guide

The second aspect of peace is that it guides, just like a prophet's ministry gives direction and guidance to the church. *"And let the peace (soul harmony which comes) from Christ rule (act as umpire continually) in your hearts"* (Col. 3:15 AMP) means that God gets to call the shots. Yes, He governs us by calling the shots, but that also means He guides us as well.

Christian maturity is not becoming *in*dependent but even more *dependent* on the Lord. David is a wonderful example of dependence on God. He did not presume to know all the answers, but continually inquired of the Lord. We must guard against being blindsided by our opinions, preferences, and agendas when it comes to making decisions. Hearing God requires neutrality on our part.

Before we make a decision based strictly on the pros and cons of our intellect, we must let peace bear witness within us and let it umpire and guide us in the decisions we face. If there's peace, then we can go ahead with making the decision; if there's an internal loss of peace, then perhaps we should respect that and stop. We don't know what the future holds, but the Lord does, and He knows how to order our steps and put all the pieces in place.

The way that works for us is like this: when we're thinking about a decision we have to make, something we need to be guided in, we immediately focus on the peace within. When even a mild feeling of anxiety is present, it's a disturbance and not of God. Peace must rule within to guide us in whatever we do. A lack of peace is considered God's guidance as well.

We have to be neutral in obeying God if we expect peace to guide us. Some people say, "I want what I want, and I want it now!" They say they have "peace" about a specific situation, but that may be false peace. We can't desire to do something so badly that we bypass God—we must simply be neutral in obeying what God desires for us. We can't force the peace to be present, and we can't ignore it when it is not there.

When we're neutral to obey God, we simply have a heart to obey Him in whatever He tells us to do. And when we're neutral to the situation and only want to obey God in whatever He wants, then peace can continually guide us. We lose our peace when the answer is no. Even if it's a faint perception, we still know it's the absence of peace, and God is saying no to that particular decision.

When I had to make a serious decision about moving to Charlotte, North Carolina, I allowed peace to be my guide. As soon as I would drop down into my spirit and say, "But I want what God wants," the peace would come flooding into my heart. I knew beyond the shadow of a doubt that I was neutral about the decision, which was key for guidance to come. I had no predilection either way. I wanted what God wanted. And for guidance to be effective, that has to be the focus. Then I asked God, "Should I leave for Charlotte now?" And the peace increased.

I have lived a lifestyle of communion with God long enough to prove to me that walking in peace is more reliable than any amount of logical information. If peace guides me, then I know I'm in God's will.

When we were engaged to be married and were looking for a house in the Charlotte, North Carolina area, Jen only had a few days in Charlotte before she had to return to Waycross, Georgia, where she owned a house. Jen, Allison (Jen's daughter), and I drove all over looking for the "right" house. Nothing seemed to fit what we wanted, but we continued to stay in peace. Finally, we drove down to Rock Hill, South Carolina, which is just south of Charlotte, and pulled off I-77 onto Cherry Road. A few miles down the road, we pulled into the parking lot of a fast-food restaurant and prayed: "Lord, we don't have much time to look. Please direct us to the house You have already chosen for us."

We continued driving until we were almost at Winthrop University, and we felt led to make two left turns into an older neighborhood. There on the left-hand side of the road was a small house with grey siding with a sign that read *For Sale by Owner* in the yard. Peace flooded the car. I got out of the car and rang the doorbell. An attractive woman came to the door and asked if we could come back in 30 minutes so she could straighten things up.

When we came back and took a tour, we were amazed at how spacious and charming the house was. It had a knotty pine library with built-in bookshelves and desk, a beautiful stained glass window in the breakfast nook, and a newly added master suite. The master bath also had a stained glass window that was stunning. Jen was walking with the owner and Allison and I walked behind them. Allison tugged on my sleeve, whispering, "This is the house, this is it! Do you think Mom knows this is the house?"

The owner agreed to hold the house for two weeks contingent on Jen selling her house in Waycross. Allison and Jen returned home and Jen called two people who had expressed an interest in her house should she ever decide to sell. One person took her up on the offer and paid cash for her house two days later.

Jen and I lived in Rock Hill for a little over a year, but it was on our hearts to have my parents move from Pennsylvania so they could live with us. It was obvious that our house wouldn't work for two families. My mother's health was precarious and she couldn't do stairs, so we began searching for a house that could accommodate her needs. Jen said that she didn't want to build, which turned out to be a mistake. When we are trusting God to guide us, our own opinions can get in the way. It is much better to stay neutral and open.

Finally, after searching for six months, Jen did a search of homes under construction in the area. While searching the Internet, a house was listed by a builder in a neighborhood called "Bailiwyck." (Bailiwyck is an alternate spelling for bailiwick). When Jen showed it to me, the power of God hit us both. I said, "That's it! What does *bailiwick* mean? Look it up!"

A bailiff is an officer, similar to a sheriff, and the area of his jurisdiction is his bailiwick. It comes from Middle English *baillifwik*, from *baillif* and *wik,* "dwelling place." (It turned out, many years later, that God told us to plant a church in a building one street over from our house, located in Bailiwyck as well. Our vision for the church is to build a "dwelling place for God.")

We drove to the location, and it turned out that there were two houses being built by the contractor. We called the number on the sign in the front yard, and he met us there to show us the houses. Both houses were lovely, but we felt a stronger sense of peace rested on one of them. When we asked friends to take a look, without exception they felt a strong anointing on that same house. We let the peace of God guide us and bought the house.

Guard

The third aspect of peace is that it guards our hearts and our minds in Christ Jesus, just as a pastor is called to shepherd the flock of God. Philippians 4:7 says, *"And the peace of God, which surpasses all understanding, will guard your hearts and minds through Christ Jesus." Guard* means the Lord will keep us safe and secure in His presence regardless of external circumstances.

What Paul wrote about peace wasn't meant to be poetic words—it was meant to be an encounter with Christ. Peace guarding our heart was meant to be a supernatural experience—not a definition we merely memorize. When peace guards our heart, we can be in any type of hostile environment and perceive the external atmosphere but abide in peace within.

Some parents we know told us that their four-year-old daughter, Elena, was having difficulty going to bed at night because she was afraid. Elena received forgiveness for taking in fear and learned how to "drop down" to peace in the presence of Jesus in her heart. She later said, "I'm not afraid of going to bed or anything else because I have Jesus with me!" If children can do this, then surely we all can do it!

Go and Gather

The fourth aspect of peace is that it goes and gathers. Peace has a magnetic power to it. Abiding in Christ is something I've been walking in for quite some time now, and I've had people come up to me and just stand by me in order to feel God's peace. Even troubled congregation members will often come up and ask me, "Is it okay if I just stand by you for a minute?" They want to experience the Prince of Peace, who is with me every moment of every day.

Throughout my years of ministry, I've also had non-Christians come up to me and say, "I feel peace coming from you; I want that." It is actually a great tool for evangelism. I don't feel like I'm the most articulate person when it comes to evangelism, but when they're attracted to the peace of God within me I respond by telling them that Christ works from the inside out. I say, "You can have this same peace too. You're feeling it on the outside, but God can give it to you on the inside if you'll receive Him. Then you'll have peace with God."

We've even had unsaved people come up to us in the middle of the mall, just weeping for no apparent reason. It's because they feel the peace of God residing with us. The peace of God gathers others around us, giving them a sense of comfort and rest from the turmoil surrounding them.

Peace also draws believers together in spiritual relationships. A temporary "unity" called *project unity* occurs when people come together to complete a task, such as painting a church or going on a missions trip. However, those involved are committed only to the project, not to the *relationships*. Real unity begins when hearts are knit together in the *"bond of peace"* (Eph. 4:3). Jesus Himself gave five-fold ministers to equip believers for unity (see Eph. 4:11-13).

God draws people together in divine appointments, which may become divine connections. God brings divine connections together in divine order, and those who are knit by the Spirit can then be God's corporate vessels for His divine purposes.

The disciples waited together in the upper room and came into one accord, which is a particularly strong spiritual knitting. On the day of Pentecost, their unity was answered by a mighty outpouring of the Holy Spirit. Later in the Book of Acts, persecuted believers prayed in one accord for boldness, and *"the place where they were assembled together was shaken; and they were all filled with the Holy Spirit, and they spoke the word of God with boldness"* (Acts 4:31).

Ground

The peace of God also grounds us in our daily lives, just as a Bible teacher roots us and grounds us in God's Word. There are rich encounters we can have in God, and there is also a progressive way of practicing His presence that grounds us in the reality of His peace. Everyone knows we must practice to become good at something. We will not become an accomplished musician or athlete without discipline and commitment. Likewise, we will not become spiritually proficient unless we become determined to practice the presence of God.

At times, God visits us in beautiful, sovereign encounters in which we receive impartations of His love and peace. As wonderful as those experiences are, they are relatively rare over the course of a lifetime. How much more efficient could our spiritual growth be if we learned how to practice "spiritual experiences" on a daily basis. The greatest truth is that we can become intentional about living our Christian life, having it grounded and established in our hearts by practice.

We worked with a mother and her son, Kyle, because he was having some behavioral problems at his Christian school. Kyle learned how to deal effectively with his emotions before they erupted into outbursts. More importantly, he worked through a course of daily prayer for two months, allowing the Lord to show him root issues contributing to his difficulties at school. We call it "intentional sanctification." Deal with problems *before* they happen! Within 60 days, Kyle was a changed young man, and his mother and the school were thrilled. He became grounded and established in peace by "walking it out."

A Christian wife we know was in a difficult marriage. Over the course of many years, she practiced forgiveness and peace. Through much practice, she became rooted and grounded in peace so that she was able to keep her peace in circumstances that would cause most Christians to be emotionally wrecked. She practiced dropping down and let a river of peace flood the atmosphere in her home. Her husband was gloriously saved without her saying a word to him about Jesus or leaving tracts around the house.

Too many believers career from crisis to crisis and say they are in spiritual warfare. Most of the time, the only issue is their own carnality. Fortunately, when we learn to use our God-tools, we can avert trouble before it happens. Doesn't that sound like a better way to live?

We prayed for a woman at a meeting on the coast of North Carolina, asking God for an emotional healing directed toward forgiving her mother. She wept as we led her through prayer. Then she said, "I've been harboring this bitterness for far too long. I think this is the first time I've ever felt peace in my life." She later notified us that she had supernaturally lost around 100 pounds, and the weight was continuing to come off.

Over the next year, people she didn't even know came up to her, saying, "I have clothes to give you." They supplied her with a new wardrobe in the process of everything else that was taking place—it was a double blessing. The peace of God grounded her, causing supernatural blessing to come to so many aspects of her life.

So God's peace roots us in reality, as well as rooting us in the present. When we have the peace of God ruling and reigning in our life, we are firmly planted, unshakable, and always abounding in the work of God. So peace governs, guides, guards, goes and gathers, and grounds us in the presence of God.

STUCK IN TRAFFIC

Jennifer and I did traveling ministry in the past, going from church to church without much downtime in between. On one occasion we were driving from a meeting in West Haven, Connecticut to Manchester, approximately an hour's drive. It was about 10:00 p.m., and we were tired. We turned onto I-84 on the last leg of our trip and were one exit away from the hotel where we were staying for the night. Suddenly the traffic came to a complete standstill. All eight lanes were blocked off and we watched as the police put up yellow crime scene tape.

Jennifer looked at me, and we were both thinking the same thing—*we were just one mile from a bed*. Our initial reaction was to become worried and move out of peace because of the circumstances. But we said, "No, we're going to practice what we preach." So we just yielded to the peace within.

We said to ourselves, "This place of peace is where we live. This is where we've learned everything. We're not going to get involved in this. We're going to Him." And when we dropped down and allowed the peace to rule even though our heads had no clue as to what was going to transpire, an abiding peace invaded our hearts.

Inexplicably, I felt led to move one car length over, which is ridiculous with hundreds of stalled cars all around us. I didn't think, "I'm going to change lanes." I was paying more attention to my gut than my head. I wasn't looking for a second opinion—I was looking for God's opinion.

When I pulled the car into the other lane, we were right next to the concrete median wall where the tape was attached. Almost immediately a policeman came and pulled back the tape, allowing eight or nine cars to pass through, then he put the tape back, stopping traffic once again. Our car was the last one to go through. We heard on the news the following day that the highway was closed until 6:00 a.m. because the police were looking for shell casings from a shootout that started in Hartford and continued as the perpetrators roared down the expressway.

It was such a supernatural event. We believe the officer might have been an angel who opened the way and let us through that night. But we honored the Lord in the midst of what seemed to be contrary circumstances. When we chose to drop down into the peace of God, we were essentially saying, "I want Your rule regardless of the circumstances." And in honoring God, we received a wonderful blessing from Him. God says, *"For those who honor Me I will honor"* (1 Sam. 2:30).

CHAPTER 10

GROWING IN THE GRACE AND KNOWLEDGE OF GOD

By Dennis

A TWO-PRONGED APPROACH

When concluding his second letter, Peter exhorted his readers to *"grow in the grace and knowledge of our Lord and Savior Jesus Christ"* (2 Pet. 3:18). Grace and knowledge must go hand in hand in order for genuine spiritual development. We cannot grow in one without the other, or we will find ourselves unbalanced in all that we do.

Grace increases the more we know God. The more we know Him, the more grace we receive from Him. We grow in grace as God owns more of us and we grow in knowledge of Him through intimate relationship. Paul said, *"But if one loves God truly [with affectionate reverence, prompt obedience, and grateful recognition of His blessing], he is known by God [recognized as worthy of His intimacy and love, and he is owned by Him]"* (1 Cor. 8:3 AMP).

God's grace is the personal presence of Jesus empowering us to be all that we were created to be and to do all that we are called to do. Christ lives His life through us by *grace* (see Gal. 2:20-21).

When we yield to the Lord and allow Him to work through His grace within our heart, then He will cause us to *want* to do His will for our lives (see Phil. 2:13). That's supernatural empowerment, which is the opposite of trying to do things *for* God. If you feel that what we're writing about in this book is too hard to do, you are not factoring in the grace of God. His grace changes everything. Only Jesus can live the Christian life through us. We can't do it for Him. Therefore, our task is to simply get out of His way so He can live through us.

> *I have been crucified with Christ and I no longer live, but Christ lives in me. The life I live in the body, I live by faith in the Son of God, who loved me and gave Himself for me. I do not set aside the grace of God, for if righteousness could be gained through the law, Christ died for nothing!* (Galatians 2:20-21 NIV)

When God revealed Himself as Jehovah-Shalom to Gideon, there was an empowerment that took place from the manifestation of God's presence. Gideon went from a place of hiding in fear and intimidation to a place of God-confidence, trusting in His security because of the manifestation of who He was. We need to experience God like this.

WORKING IN WILLPOWER

Paul cautioned the Colossians about the practice of "will worship." Will worship is man-made religion driven by evil spirits. Sadly, far too many Christians are captive to religion and live far short of what God intended for us. Paul wrote:

> *Wherefore if ye be dead with Christ from the rudiments of the world, why, as though living in the world, are ye subject to ordinances, (Touch not; taste not; handle not; which all are to perish with the using;) after the commandments and doctrines of men? Which things have indeed a shew of wisdom in will worship, and humility, and neglecting of the body; not in any honour to the satisfying of the flesh* (Colossians 2:20-23 KJV).

Not all religious activity and worship is acceptable to God. Jesus says true worship must be in "spirit and in truth" (see John 4:24). First of all, the source must be right. The Spirit of God must initiate true worship. Second, the word *truth* means real, ideal, or genuine. Worship must flow through us as we make a real spiritual connection with God.

> *But the hour is coming, and now is, when the true worshipers will worship the Father in spirit and truth; for the Father is seeking such to worship Him. God is Spirit, and those who worship Him must worship in spirit and truth* (John 4:23-24).

Religious spirits hitchhike on religious rituals. They enslave and condemn through philosophies and traditions of man. Both *elements* and *rudiments* in Galatians 4:3 and Colossians 2:8 are *stoicheion* in the Greek, referring to Gentile cults and Jewish theories and philosophies called "philosophy and vain deceit." Paul's use of *stoicheion* indicates that animistic or demonic spirits ally with religious rituals and traditions.[1] Evil spirits use the rituals of the law to bring bondage, but life in Christ brings freedom.

> *Even so we, when we were children, were in bondage under the elements of the world* (Galatians 4:3).

> *But now after you have known God, or rather are known by God, how is it that you turn again to the weak and beggarly elements, to which you desire again to be in bondage?* (Galatians 4:9)

> *Beware lest any man spoil you through philosophy and vain deceit, after the tradition of men, after the rudiments of the world, and not after Christ* (Colossians 2:8 KJV).

Three types of false worship are: (1) vain worship, which is based on the traditions of man rather than God. It does not come from the Spirit (see Matt. 15:7-9). (2) Ignorant worship does not understand the true nature of God or the worship He desires. Paul admonished the religious Athenians for ignorant worship: *"I perceive that in all things you are very religious; for as I was passing through and considering the objects of your worship, I even found an altar with this inscription: TO THE UNKNOWN GOD. Therefore, the One whom you worship without knowing, Him I proclaim to you"* (Acts 17:22-23). (3) Will worship is self-imposed rather than God-directed. The source of will worship is human willpower rather than the Holy Spirit.

Religious spirits can hitchhike on human willpower. They cause bondage and use rituals, laws, and traditions to oppress us (see Gal. 4:3, 9). The Holy Spirit leads us gently, whereas religious spirits drive and condemn (see Col. 2:8). Paul said, *"If you died with Christ from the basic principles of the world, why, as though living in the world, do you subject yourselves to regulations—'Do not touch, do not taste, do not handle'"* (Col. 2:20-21).

We must yield to the grace of God and stop trying in our own strength. When we strive, we cease walking in the empowering presence of Christ within us.

One strategy of the enemy in the end times is to wear out the people of God. Unfortunately, the church is just as stressed as the world. We are not called to religion, we are called to relationship. We are not called to bondage but to freedom. When we get caught up in rituals and traditions, we fail to enter into the supernatural joy and peace that is the birthright of every Christian. When we are walking in the will of God, heaven can manifest on earth. We are aligned with God and He orders our life.

A supernatural exchange must take place, a spirit-to-Spirit connection whereby we feel energized by God's presence. We need the reality of the peace of God in our lives, not the counterfeit peace the world gives. Again, it's not how much Bible knowledge we have; it is about the level of peace we walk in on a consistent basis.

THE GOD OF PEACE

We grow in the grace and knowledge of God when we yield to God's grace and are obedient to His Word. We must not focus on the things of this world or we will not be able to abide in peace. We should lift our gaze higher to the heavenly realm. In Philippians 4:7-9, Paul says:

> *The peace of God, which surpasses all understanding, will guard your hearts and minds through Christ Jesus. Finally, brethren, whatever things are true, whatever things are noble, whatever things are just, whatever things are pure, whatever things are lovely, whatever things are of good report, if there is any virtue and if there is anything praiseworthy—meditate on these things. The things which you learned and received and heard and saw in me, these do, and the God of peace will be with you.*

Paul wanted the Philippians to emulate his life and character. He wasn't exhorting the church to do something he himself wasn't practicing. The Bible contains many promises of God that are conditional. In this passage of Scripture, the Lord promises the peace of God will guard our heart and mind. Forgiveness is the God-tool that keeps our heart cleansed of negative emotions and restores our peace. The first key for guarding our mind is taking responsibility for our thought life, and Paul tells us to focus on things that are:

- True: things that are real, genuine, and authentic. Don't lie.

- Noble: things of good character, principled, and honorable. Don't dishonor God or others.

- Just: things that are upright, virtuous, faultless, and guiltless. Don't spin the truth or manipulate.

- Pure: things that are clean or untainted with evil. Don't engage in evil thoughts or ways.

- Lovely: things that are of a great moral or spiritual beauty. Don't be unkind.

- Good report: things that give hope for a good future. Don't be negative.

- Virtue: things that have life-giving anointing. Don't tolerate control, manipulation, or agendas (soul ties). All of these emanate death rather than life.

- Praiseworthy: things that express approval, admiration, commendation, or praise. Don't engage in gossip or slander.

We must be victorious within before we can win the battles without. Therefore, we must avoid evil in us to wage war against the forces of evil in the world. The Lord promises us that the God of Peace will be with us if we take responsibility for keeping the doors of our emotions and mind shut to the enemy. The God of Peace will crush the enemy beneath our feet (see Rom. 16:20).

We can apply two simple tests to determine whether thoughts are godly or not. First, test the words themselves. Does it sound like something God would say? The real you is a new creation who loves God and His Word. Don't accept anything from a source other than God. Second, how does it make you feel? If the nature of God, the fruit of the Spirit, isn't on the thought, don't accept it. The source is wrong. If the thought is a simple distraction, just take it captive to the obedience of Christ by releasing it to Christ within. If you feel a negative emotion in your gut, forgiveness will restore your peace. Then you have authority to renounce the thought.

Paul wrote a letter to the believers in Philippi while he was imprisoned—hardly circumstances in which to rejoice. And yet, Philippians is the epistle of joy and fellowship. Chapter 2 instructs the church how to overcome rivalry and jealousy, killers of fellowship and unity, while chapter 4 gives the antidote for worry. The second key for guarding our mind is to conquer our tendency to worry. Worry is a sin that comes from the kingdom of fear. It is impossible to worry and have peace at the same time. They are mutually exclusive (see Phil. 4:6).

The world is full of negativity. The news media thrives on fear mongering. The headlines are filled with bad news. The words and actions of people, both in and out of the church, are often petty and cruel. How casually believers gossip about one another and leaders instead of praying for them. It is no secret that, when a leader falls, the church is quick to criticize but slow to pray.

How different these behaviors are from what Paul instructs. Do we want joy and peace or a bad attitude and worry? So how does Paul say we can overcome? Focus on those things that are true, noble, pure, lovely, of good report, virtuous, and praiseworthy. We must also keep our thoughts focused on the positive, not the negative. Release those things that trouble you into the hands of God and you will feel His peace.

When we trust in God, we have peace. When we focus on the goodness of God with a heart of gratitude and are kind to one another, we experience joy. As we do this, then the "God of Peace will be with" us, Paul says. The God of peace who brings order out of chaos is not far away or unconcerned—He is with us, dwelling within us.

If we are going to move into a deeper revelation of the God of Peace, then we must put the Scriptures into practice. We only really know the Scriptures that we live. We may have a revelation of the God of Peace, but revelation must impact our lives or it's just information. Even if we already have some revelation, it can always go deeper and deeper. We have a responsibility to apply Christian discipline in our life. In other words, when we learn that peace is always available, we can choose to practice it or continue to let carnality run our life. We can't trust God and be stressed. It is impossible to have stress and peace at the same time.

We've noticed a number of well-known leaders in the body of Christ who seem to live in a high level of stress. Our level of stress is determined by how we handle the people and circumstances of life. Everybody has trials and tribulation in this world. Life is always a mixture of good and bad at any given time. We will never have a perfect life this side of heaven. What makes the difference is whether we react in our own strength or depend on God's strength. If we are in control, we feel stressed. When the God of Peace prevails, we rest in Him. That makes all the difference in the world.

The God of Peace will guard our hearts and our minds in Christ Jesus. We don't have to wrestle with unpleasant thoughts. One strategy is to drop down in prayer and release thoughts to Christ within until we get peace. For those who struggle with their thought life on a regular basis, another strategy is to refuse to accept intrusive thoughts. You are a new creation in Christ. That's the real you, the one who loves God and loves His Word. The new creation always agrees with God. Therefore, if you hear a disturbing thought in your head, if it doesn't sound like something God would say, renounce it and refuse to pay attention to it. It doesn't matter if the thought comes from you or from the enemy, if God isn't saying it you don't want it. You can even say (aloud or silently), "That's not me," meaning the new creation you.

This is why Paul tells us to think on things that are pure, lovely, and are of good report. It is a very good quality to see things around us as half full, not half empty. Faultfinding is not a gift. We don't have to be saved to see what is wrong with someone or something. A true gift is the ability to see the potential in spite of the dirt. A gold miner digs in the dirt all day long, but his focus is on the gold, not on the dirt. We must have the same attitude as a gold miner and focus on the potential in individuals.

> More churches have been destroyed by the accuser of the brethren and faultfinding than by either immorality or misuse of church funds. So prevalent is this influence in our society that, among many, faultfinding has been elevated to the status of a "ministry!"[2]

Is God not able to change people if we pray for them with compassionate hearts? He may begin by changing us in the process. Instead of having a critical spirit, we should become a redemption-oriented people and focus on the gold in others. Redemption is the name of the game, from start to finish.

It is ironic that the church has faith that God can redeem any sinner, no matter how deeply they are mired in sin. Could God save and change that prostitute? Of course! Could God save that drug addict and set them free? Of course! However, the body of Christ is prone to be far less tolerant of brothers and sisters in Christ. There seems to be a prevalent attitude toward fellow Christians that "they should know better." The truth is that only God can change people, both saved and unsaved. That is why He tells us to pray for one another.

Many years ago, I (Dennis) heard the story of the "pea revealer." Little Johnny had a strict father who insisted that his children eat their peas. Johnny didn't like peas, so he avoided eating them whenever possible. One day, Johnny's brother, Tom, noticed an untouched mound of peas on his brother's plate and said, "Dad, look! Johnny's not eating his peas!" However, Tom had a friend visiting at dinnertime one evening. Uh, oh! Tom noticed his friend wasn't eating his peas, so he slid the corner of his napkin over and covered his friend's peas. He did for his friend what he wouldn't do for his own brother.

True discernment comes from the place of peace and love. Love precedes peace and peace precedes our perception of the people around us. God is love in us. When we yield to Him, we experience peace. Only when we have peace are we able to see clearly. To have the eyes of Jesus, we must first have the heart of Jesus.

When we operate in real spiritual discernment, we are aware of the presence of God in every situation. Too many believers minimize God and maximize evil. However, God is omnipresent; He is everywhere. There are many more angels than there are demons in the world. We must have eyes to see how big God is compared to all that is wrong.

The king of Syria was making war against Israel, and Gehazi, the servant of Elisha, was terrified. The Syrian army completely surrounded the city of Dothan. To bring peace to his heart, Elisha prayed, *"Lord, I pray, open his eyes that he may see."* Suddenly, Gehazi was able to see the angelic host, *"And behold, the mountain was full of horses and chariots of fire all around Elisha"* (2 Kings 6:17).

We should be so optimistic we could see the worst of the worst and believe that person or circumstance could change. God is raising up people, like Joshua and Caleb, who focus on the positive and are confident in their God. Joshua and Caleb were part of the band of 12 spies sent into the Promised Land to bring back a report about the land (see Num. 13:1-33). When 10 of the spies brought back an evil report, they infected the whole congregation with the disease of unbelief. The children of Israel were unable to receive the good report given by Joshua and Caleb. Because of this sin, the children of Israel wandered in the wilderness for 40 years and died without setting foot in the Promised Land.

However, Joshua and Caleb stood strong and proclaimed that God was more than able to help them take the land. Out of all the children of Israel present that day, only these two men were eventually allowed to enter the land. Unlike the spies who returned from spying out the Promised Land with an evil report, we should be like Joshua and Caleb who *"had a different spirit"* (Num. 14:24). Observe that the Bible says their *spirit* was different, not their opinion. When we give in to the report of the enemy, we make ourselves vulnerable to his spiritual influence.

Our lives need to demonstrate this in practice as we trust in God. When we have ears to hear the good reports, the God of Peace will be with us. However, if we get hung up on what is wrong, we'll lose our peace and our ability to discern as well. Receiving the "good reports" of God will be essential for victory in the days ahead. Those things that you have learned, received, heard, and saw in us—do. And as you emulate our life and character, then the God of Peace will be with you (see Phil. 4:8-9).

THE FIVE Gs OF GRACE

God is calling each of us to grow in the grace and knowledge of God. Unless God empowers us by His grace, we will never know the fullness of Christ. But before we can evaluate whether or not we're growing in grace, we must first explain what grace is not.

Grace is not head knowledge. We can know *about* God yet never come into intimate communion with Him. All our knowledge of God should lead us to a heart of worship, seeking Christ and relying on Him throughout our day. Growing in grace is not growing in our gifts, even though God gives them to us. And just because we *think* we're growing in grace doesn't mean it is true. However, there is internal evidence that can verify whether or not we are *truly* growing in the grace of God. We call these the five Gs of grace.

Govern

Colossians 3:15 says we should let the peace of God rule, or govern, our hearts. Growing in grace means that we trust the Lord more and more in our lives. We no longer feel we need to be in control, but we give ourselves completely to God, trusting that *He* has everything under control. We can say with increasing confidence that Jesus is truly becoming Lord of our life.

As the peace of God governs us, a foundation of trust is established in our heart. We do not trust ourselves as much as we used to, but we let the God of Peace rule our heart and all of our decision-making processes. We trust ourselves less and God more. Again, this doesn't mean we trust perfectly every day, but at least we quickly return to the place of peace when we step out of it momentarily.

> *He who dwells in the secret place of the Most High shall abide under the shadow of the Almighty. I will say of the Lord, "He is my refuge and my fortress; My God, in Him I will trust"* (Psalm 91:1-2).

In addition to becoming more adept at letting the peace of God govern us, our zeal for God grows. Our zeal is directed toward our relationship with God Himself, not ministry or religion. As we turn to God and allow His peace to govern our heart, then the God of Peace will rule in all situations with all people. His peace also brings transformation, order, and harmony in the hearts and lives of others just by contact with us.

When I was a new believer, finances were tight as God began to rebuild my life from the ruin I had made of it. I was having trouble with the transmission of my car and I only had $12.85 in my checking account. Although I was well aware of how expensive work on a transmission could be, with the confidence of a baby Christian just learning about God, I said in my heart, "Well, God, how are You going to get me out of this one?"

I knew He would come through for me somehow. So I took my car to the shop and the mechanic took a look at it. He said, "We don't need to replace the transmission. All it needs is a bottle of this transmission fluid." I asked him how much the fluid was. He replied, "Twelve dollars."

Guide

The peace of God should also umpire the daily decisions we make. An umpire calls the shots in a baseball game. Players may argue with him, but the umpire ultimately has the final authority. In other words, what the umpire says goes. We should never make decisions out of fear or any other negative emotion but out of a place of peace. When we make a decision without peace, things can't turn out well because our motivation is all wrong. Any time we make a decision out of guilt, anger, or some other toxic emotion, anything other than the peace of God, then God is not umpiring in our lives. He is sitting on the bench, and we are in control.

It is important that we have peace before making any decision. As we grow in the grace of God, we'll begin to make better and better decisions in our lives, letting His peace rule and reign. We'll be guided more by His peace than by anything else in our lives. It is incredible that when we give ourselves to God and His ways, He begins to guide us by the gentle hand of His peace.

A friend of ours, who is a very successful businessman, testifies that he makes all his business decisions by staying in peace. If two contracts are placed on his desk, he doesn't rely on logical reasoning but relies on the peace of God to make his decisions. As a result, God has greatly blessed him financially.

Go and Gather

There is a gathering aspect to the peace of God that brings peace to those around us, both to believers and unbelievers alike. No matter where we go in our lives, peace gives us influence with those around us. Whether we are at home or in the workplace, the gospel of peace surrounds us and draws others into what God has for them.

God brings peace to unbelievers, wooing and gathering the unsaved to the Lord. When we are at the grocery store, in restaurants, or at the mall, we deliberately release rivers of love and peace to certain individuals as the Lord leads. It is a common occurrence for people to be drawn to us. Often they walk over and talk with us with completely open hearts and tears in their eyes. When there is opportunity, we speak with them about the Lord.

A young man, a backslidden believer, had gotten involved with drugs and was serving a two-year sentence in prison. His Christian parents sent him a copy of our book *Live Free*. He read the book and put it into practice in his own life while incarcerated. We were with his parents and they got him on the phone to tell us what had been happening. The peace he was experiencing was so strong that other prisoners were being drawn to him like a magnet. He was leading them to the Lord and teaching them how to have peace in the midst of a difficult situation.

When we win the lost to the Lord, they experience *"peace with God"* for the first time (Rom. 5:1). As they grow in the faith and become Christian disciples, they discover how to maintain the peace of God in their lives (see Col. 3:15). We encourage them to become part of an assembly of believers so they can have fellowship with other believers in the *"bond of peace"* (Eph. 4:3).

When they gain spiritual prowess, they come to know the God of Peace who crushes the enemy beneath their feet (see Rom. 16:20).

Peace also gathers those who are already saved. When my son Jason was very young, he loved the peaceful atmosphere of my prayer time. He enjoyed snuggling up close to me when I was praying. One time he mentioned that he didn't want to go to church prayer meetings anymore. So I asked him, "What are they saying?"

He responded, "Oh, it's not what they're saying. I just feel anger and fear in the atmosphere. It doesn't feel like it does when you are praying." He enjoyed being in the presence of peace.

We are growing in grace when we deal quickly with negative emotions so they don't "poison" the atmosphere around us. We must pray in faith, not pray our worries. In our relationships with others, we must keep the walls down by practicing a forgiveness lifestyle.

A woman in the first church I planted once said she liked to come over and stand by me at church because the peace felt so wonderful. Some believers from another part of the county visited our church not long ago and spontaneously commented that they could feel a powerful sense of unity in our assembly. They were sensing the *bond of peace* (Eph. 4:3). Peace has a magnetic atmosphere to it, for both unbelievers and believers alike. The peace of God goes and gathers.

Guard

When peace guards us, we have no need for walls of self-protection. Peace is evidence of the reign of Christ. When we are in peace, we can hear from the Lord and He will give us wisdom.

Stress is impossible when we are in peace. If we lose our peace and feel negative emotions, forgiveness will instantly restore peace. We can respond in the fruit of the Sprit rather than react in carnality.

One of the evidences we are growing in grace is that we begin to experience peace in the midst of the troubles of life. We are also increasingly able to stay in peace regardless of the petty annoyances and inconveniences that occur. This is where the rubber meets the road. Disasters don't happen too often, but the little aggravations come almost daily.

When we are growing in the grace of God, difficult circumstances don't bother us as much as they used to. As our spiritual strength increases, we become less likely to magnify the trials we face. Instead, we can focus on the positive in the midst of the negative. We will become people who know how to let the peace of God guard our hearts and our lives. Did the peace of God consistently guard my heart today? The answer to that question will determine whether or not we're growing in grace.

Ground

When we become rooted and grounded in the peace of God, we experience less anxiety and stress, and this is another evidence that we are growing in grace. As we continue to grow in grace, we become more and more sanctified, and our whole spirit, soul, and body will be impacted by the peace of God (see 1 Thess. 5:23).

We become grounded through practice, practice, practice. Have you practiced dropping down and relying on the Lord today? Are you improving? There are two twin disciplines in the discipleship of peace. First, we must practice living in peace through a forgiveness lifestyle. Second, when we have peace, we can both discern the atmosphere around us and successfully resist any negatives we sense in the atmosphere.

When we can discern the atmosphere because we have peace in our heart, God can give us wisdom to know what to do in each specific situation. When we are at peace, we can hear from God more clearly. Difficult people and trying circumstances will become opportunities for practice so we become more grounded in grace. When we are grounded in peace, it becomes part of our spiritual foundation.

Stina was diligently practicing what she had learned from us. Driving in Boston traffic one day, a truck in front of her drove through a red light. Without thinking, she just followed it. Once she realized what she had done, she stopped. A nearby policeman didn't notice the truck, but did see Stina and was yelling at her as he walked toward her car. She was so distraught that her hands started shaking. "Oh, no! Oh, no! I have to do what Dennis and Jennifer taught me!" she said. So she "dropped down" to Jesus in her heart.

Stina instantly felt supernatural peace, and she noticed her hands stopped shaking immediately. She then started releasing shalom and love to the angry policeman. By the time he got to her car, he had stopped yelling, and said, "Oh, lady. I hate going to court. Just go." And he motioned for her to drive away. The moral of the story is not how to get out of a ticket, but to show that peace is practical and it grounds us.

Peace must become a way of life so we will be established on a strong spiritual foundation. The world has tribulation, but we have overcome the world through the peace of Christ (see John

16:33). As our sanctification increases with additional areas of our life given to God, we gain spiritual strength—evidence that we are growing in the grace of God. God is now in charge of more of our life.

As we can see, noticeable internal and external evidences are proof we are growing in the grace and knowledge of God. We don't have to guess about how we are doing, but we can know by the five-fold evidence of growing in grace that is visible in our lives.

PRACTICE AND REVIEW

The peace of God ministers in five arenas of life. On your Daily Rule of Peace Chart (below), keep track of your progress. Don't expect perfection, but rejoice in improvement. Whenever you lose your peace, forgiveness (or release) will restore it. If you really blow it, receive forgiveness and start practicing peace again. Forgiveness removes anything momentarily interrupting a sense of the presence of God and awareness of His peace: *"For He Himself is our peace"* (Eph. 2:14).

Peace Governs

When Jesus is ruling or governing your life, you always feel peace in your heart. When you have peace, you have the assurance that God is in control of your life. If you lose your peace, forgive (or release it to God if it's a circumstance) and you will instantly feel peace again.

If you feel a negative emotion but don't give in to it, it is temptation, not sin. You can simply release it. For example, suppose a co-worker does something irritating; you may momentarily feel irritation but quickly release it into the hands of God and get your peace back. However, if you become angry and stew on it for a while, you need to forgive the person and receive forgiveness for letting the negative emotion stay too long.

Let the peace of God rule (Colossians 3:15).

Peace Guides

Before you make any decision, first be sure you are neutral so you are able to hear from God. Begin by releasing preferences or opinions into the hands of God. When you are neutral, inquire in silent prayer. Next, present the choices one at a time to the Lord. You will sense an increased anointing on God's choice. If you don't sense the presence of God on any option, wait. The timing may be wrong, or God may have another plan He has yet to reveal. Never go ahead with something if you lose your peace.

Let the peace (soul harmony which comes) from Christ rule (act as umpire continually) (Colossians 3:15 AMP).

Peace Goes and Gathers

Peace is like a magnetic force that attracts people to the presence of God. When you have supernatural peace, you are a force for good in the world and unity in the church. Have you been a magnetic force, or have you pushed people away from God?

How beautiful are the feet of those who preach the gospel of peace (Romans 10:15).

Keep the unity of the Spirit in the bond of peace (Ephesians 4:3).

Peace Guards

When you have peace, you are fully under God's control. In Luke 4, Jesus walked through the crowd who wanted to push Him off a cliff because He was fully submitted to Father God. When you stay in peace, you don't need to put up walls, be stressed, or have negative emotions, and you can respond out of peace rather than react. Peace is powerful protection!

> *The peace of God, which surpasses all understanding, will guard your hearts and minds* (Philippians 4:7).

> *You will keep him in perfect peace, whose mind [creative imagination] is stayed on You* (Isaiah 26:3).

> *The God of peace will crush Satan under your feet* (Romans 16:20).

Peace Grounds

Practice makes permanent. The more you practice, the better you will become at maintaining peace as a lifestyle. Peace will keep you grounded in a life submitted to God. Peace will become a sure foundation for your Christian life. Remember, every baby step of obedience builds spiritual strength!

> *The kingdom of God is...righteousness, peace, and joy* (Romans 14:17).

> *I've told you all this so that trusting Me, you will be unshakable and assured, deeply at peace. In this godless world you will continue to experience difficulties. But take heart! I've conquered the world* (John 16:33 MSG).

But solid food belongs to those who are of full age, that is, those who by reason of use have their senses exercised to discern both good and evil (Hebrews 5:14).

We have included a daily chart so you can assess yourself (see below).

DAILY RULE OF PEACE

THE FIVE-FOLD MINISTRY OF PEACE

1. PEACE GOVERNS: CIRCUMSTANCES AND PEOPLE

Let the peace of God rule (Col. 3:15).

Over all circumstances, with all people.

Let the peace of God rule!

If it's temptation, release before sinning.

Yes _____ No _____

If you sin, forgive God, self, and others.

Yes _____ No _____

2. PEACE GUIDES: DECISIONS

Let the peace (soul harmony which comes) *from Christ rule* (act as umpire continually) (Col. 3:15).

Make all decisions with peace.

Let peace be the umpire!

No decision without peace today:

Yes _____ No _____

3. PEACE GOES AND GATHERS: FOR THE SAVED AND THE UNSAVED

Wear shoes of peace (see Eph. 6:15).

Maintain the bond of peace (see Eph. 4:3).

Proclaim peace (see Rom. 10:15).

Influence in the home, at work, in all arenas.

Wear shoes of peace, proclaim peace, and maintain bonds of peace.

My influence:

Positive _____ Negative _____

Was influenced:

Positive _____ Negative _____

4. PEACE GUARDS: PROTECTION AND VICTORY

The peace of God, which surpasses all understanding, will guard your hearts and minds (Philippians 4:7).

You will keep him in perfect peace, whose mind (creative imagination) *is stayed on You* (Isaiah 26:3).

The God of peace will crush Satan under your feet (Romans 16:20).

Peace guarded my heart and mind today.

The peace of God will guard your hearts and minds.

No walls:

Yes _____ No _____

No stress:

Yes _____ No _____

No negative emotions:

Yes _____ No _____

Responded, not reacted:

Yes _____ No _____

5. PEACE GROUNDS: PRACTICE, PRACTICE, PRACTICE!

The kingdom of God is...righteousness, peace and joy (Romans 14:17).

I've told you all this so that trusting me, you will be unshakable and assured, deeply at peace. In this godless world you will continue to experience difficulties. But take heart! I've conquered the world (John 16:33 MSG).

But solid food belongs to those who are of full age, that is, those who by reason of use have their senses exercised to discern both good and evil (Hebrews 5:14).

Practice makes permanent!

Did you practice regularly today?

The kingdom of God is peace. Peace needs to be practiced so you will be grounded on a strong foundation. The world has tribulation, but God has removed its power to harm you (see John 16:33).

Have you practiced?
Yes _____ No _____

Are you improving?
Yes _____ No _____

ENDNOTES

1. Elements [stoicheion in Greek] "translates a Greek word, which originally referred to the triangle on a sundial for determining time by a shadow-line. From there it came to be applied to a going in order, advancing in steps or rows, elementary beginnings, and learning the letters of the alphabet. In NT usage, the word refers to the elementary principles of the OT (Heb. 5:12), the rudiments of both Jewish and Gentile religion (here and Col. 2:8, 20) and the material elements of the universe (2 Pet. 3:10, 12). "Paul's use of the same word in v. 9 ('the weak and beggarly elements'), along with its usage in Col. 2, lends further insight into 'elements.' He teaches that spirits of the animistic or demonic dimension (v. 8) find easy allegiance with the rituals and philosophies of human religion and tradition. Hence, the elements of the world are actually evil spirits that use the rituals of the Law (v. 10) to enslave and condemn." [Footnote for Galatians 4:3, *Spirit-Filled Life Bible*, ed. Jack Hayford, 1777.

2. Francis Frangipane, February 5, 2005. Accessed on May 23, 2014, from http://www.dailychristianquote.com/francis-frangipane-19/.

CHAPTER 11

AN EVER-INCREASING TRUST

BY DENNIS

A REVELATION OF THE GOD OF PEACE

When I was a young Christian and first began the process of simple prayer, I came before the Lord with an attitude of honor, meaning to have high respect, great esteem, and courteous regard for Him. I came as the lesser with a greater. I never approached Him to ask Him for "things" or have an expectation that He should serve me; I only wanted more of Him. To this day, He is my Master and I am His servant. He is my Teacher and I am His disciple. Therefore, I wait for Him to initiate and allow Him to guide me any way He desires.

The Lord God has given Me the tongue of a disciple and of one who is taught, that I should know how

to speak a word in season to him who is weary. He
wakens Me morning by morning, He wakens My ear
to hear as a disciple [as one who is taught] (Isaiah 50:4
AMP).

Because I honored Him as a Person who was present with
me, I found that I could also sense different nuances of His
presence. Prayer is not an action, it is communion; therefore, I
desired to experience His nature in whatever way He chose to
manifest Himself to me. I would then commit to enjoy Him in
that particular aspect of His divine nature for a period of time
until He unveiled a different facet of Himself. I allowed God to
be the initiator on each subject.

As a relatively new believer, I discovered this was how the
Holy Spirit taught Charles Finney (1792-1875). Finney said
that a particular facet of the divine nature was his only when it
became a reality instead of a theory. From that time to the present day, I still follow this practice.[1]

I later discovered that our areas of greatest spiritual strength
are directly correlated to those relationships in which we have
walked with Him. For example, to know God as our Shepherd,
we must walk in the relationship of a sheep in the care of the
Good Shepherd. Throughout the day, I cultivated an awareness
of my Shepherd who led me to rest in Him and quench my spiritual thirst in the river of peace. During times of uncertainty or
apparent danger, I sensed that He was with me to guide me and
keep me safe. It was a real relationship like that of John, who
testified that he still fellowshipped with the ascended Christ (see
1 John 1:1-4).

To know God as our Healer, we must fellowship with Him as our Jehovah-Rapha. To know God as our Peace, we must walk with Him in that relationship as well. I had experienced so much rejection that it was my greatest weakness, so God revealed Himself to me as "love and acceptance." He so thoroughly purged out rejection that acceptance is now my strongest anointing. If we have an area of deficiency in our lives, God will become our sufficiency when we commune with Him and allow Him to fill our need.

The way I approach it is like this: I come into the presence of God, as I do every morning, and I just close my eyes and drop down to my heart to experience His peace. I come before Him with the attitude, "God, I'm here to honor You and experience Your peace this morning. Reveal Yourself to me." I just sit quietly before Him while enjoying His presence.

I pay attention to the nuances of His nature that I sense in the atmosphere. This is how we learn the "silent whispers" of the Holy Spirit. Do I sense love, strength, healing power, comfort, or refreshing? Over time I have learned to recognize many subtleties of the Spirit, but He is always with me to teach me even more. He often speaks a word to my spirit. Other times He quickens a Scripture to my heart and I yield and enter into it, allowing myself time to eat and assimilate what He is saying. That is my "daily portion" of bread from heaven (see Matt. 6:11). It is the meal the Lord has prepared for me.

I find that God reveals Himself progressively to us. He doesn't show up in His fullness all at once but gradually reveals little by little who He is. We receive an increasing revelation of the Person of God. We don't just read a Scripture about Him one time and then walk away thinking that we have a full revelation of that aspect of His being. Rather, we need to eat it, digest it, and assimilate it so it becomes a part of us. We don't want a revelation of God to be just a concept, but a reality we experience in our everyday lives.

As our revelation of the Person of God grows, we grow in grace. Only by absorbing the substance, the divine nature of who God is, can we grow spiritually. We go from faith to faith and glory to glory. We are transformed from one degree of glory to the next. This change takes place as we consistently walk in God's grace.

THE DIFFICULTY OF TRUSTING GOD

Whenever God begins to speak to us about something, Jen and I always ask Him for wisdom because we don't want to teach theory but give practical wisdom about how spiritual truth works. Most believers have enough Bible *information*, but they don't know how to apply it to their lives.

Knowledge refers to having facts and information. Understanding adds meaning and principles to our knowledge. But wisdom adds practical application to knowledge and understanding. Wisdom reveals how I can use what I have learned. Wisdom and understanding must be added to our knowledge to have Christianity that is real.

We are committed to revealing the workable secrets for abiding in Christ. What good is our Christian faith if we can't live it out? We need relationship, not religion. Only then can we learn to fully trust God in our daily life. Too many believers have difficulty trusting God in many areas of their lives. Almost all believers know *theologically* that God is omnipresent, meaning He is present everywhere all the time, whether we feel Him not. Our awareness of Him, or the lack thereof, doesn't mean that He is not present. What we need, however, is the actual awareness of His presence moment by moment. That is the *reality* of omnipresence.

When it comes to salvation, believers generally don't have a problem believing God will come into an unbeliever's heart if they ask Him. Almost all Christians have total, implicit faith that whether we feel Him or see Him, if someone asked Jesus to come into their heart and save them, He would do that—immediately. We are totally convinced that if we receive Jesus in our hearts to forgive us from our sins He would do just that. Why? Because He's always present.

Faith may be defined as a strong or unshakeable belief in something. That is good as far as it goes, but faith by itself can be entirely mental. Even a small child may have faith that the light will come on when they push the switch up. True spiritual faith, however, engages the heart and is the gateway into experience. *Saving faith* is necessary for our initial conversion experience. We believe Jesus is present to save, and by faith we welcome Him into our heart. Our faith is rewarded by a true inner assurance that something happened because we can now sense the presence of God where before we couldn't.[2]

However, if we want to move from the mental understanding of omnipresence to live in His manifest presence, we must have *living faith*. Living faith is not a "blind faith" but a reality that can be tested. We don't have to "take it by faith" that Jesus has given us peace; we can experience peace. We don't have to believe it is possible to abide; we can experience abiding in Him.

We must learn to trust that He is present at any moment of any day if we are going to live in His presence in a more powerful way. We can't grow in the peace of God until we have confidence He is always present to bring us back to the place of peace when we lose it. This omnipresent God is available to take us from one level to the next. Nobody can argue us into another level of faith. No one can give us good enough theological reasons to cause us to automatically trust God in certain situations. Mental gymnastics don't work.

Suppose we have been looking for a new job and suddenly get two job offers. We don't have to pray, beg, or plead to receive a word or special sign from God. We only have to start moving. God can work with someone in motion. If we feel the anointing increase when we check out one possibility and the anointing diminishes when we investigate the other, or we get a check in our spirit, we have our answer. Keep moving toward the greater anointing and obey the stop signs of the Holy Spirit.

Remember, God will guide us by His peace. He will never put His supernatural peace on anything that isn't His will. We must remember, though, that it is possible to get a *false peace* that is a product of our flesh. Our flesh likes to get what it wants. "Oh," our flesh says, "I have had a hard day and deserve to eat a banana split to make myself feel better!" We might feel the peace of satisfied lust temporarily. Of course, we will pay a price later in guilt and, perhaps, putting on a few extra pounds. When we truly want God's will more than our own, we will be able to distinguish between God's peace and instant gratification.

The Stanford Marshmallow Experiment, led by psychologist Walter Mischel at Stanford University during the 1960s and 1970s, was a series of studies involving young children from ages four to six. The researcher gave each child a marshmallow (or other edible treat), saying, "I have to leave for a moment, but if you don't eat the treat until I return, I will give you another one." Then the researcher left the room for approximately 15 minutes and observed the behavior of the subject through a one-way mirror.

Most of the children stuffed the goodies into their mouths immediately. Some picked it up, licked it repeatedly, but put it back down without eating it. Very few managed to look but not touch, although the expressions on their faces reflected their internal struggle. Follow-up studies revealed that those who had been able to wait longer tended to be more successful later in life.[3] When we trust God and wait on His timing, we overcome our desire for instant gratification.

When we say we don't trust God, we really mean that we don't trust Him in a specific area or for a specific thing. We trust God because we've been born again—we trusted Him for salvation and we live a daily life of trusting Him. But when we say we are learning to trust Him in a specific area, we are really suggesting that we are more comfortable taking matters into our own hands. We're refusing to receive what is made available to us in Christ.[4]

When God showed up and said to Gideon, "Peace to you," what happened to Gideon? He was transformed from an anxious man to a man of peace. There was a transference that took place in that encounter with God. Gideon didn't just say, "Oh, what a great idea!" No, there was something he had to receive. He didn't get it just by being exposed to it. He had to open himself up and receive that revelation of Jehovah-Shalom.

THE IMPORTANCE OF RECEIVING

We start with a desire to know the God of Peace. But after the desire is present within us, we must learn to receive all God has for us. It is important to pray through doubt because we all have a tendency to doubt. We must receive forgiveness for fear, doubt, and unbelief. When any nagging thoughts of disbelief arise, we need to receive forgiveness and open to an assurance of God's faithfulness. Choosing to trust and receiving a supernatural exchange to strengthen and to build up our spirit man is of utmost importance.

We can't skip dealing with our fears because they render us incapable of going any further in God. We must overcome our fears before we can attain our dreams. Most of our worries center around things that are unattainable, unknowable, and uncontrollable. Almost everything we are afraid of falls into one of these three categories. We must face what we dread and refuse to tolerate fear in our lives.

We have a choice to make: will we yield to a faithful God or give in to one of these three fears? If we choose to yield to fear, we become an open target for the enemy and will forfeit the peace we could otherwise have. We need to release these fears into the loving hands of God. The bottom line is that we have to release control.

Bringing God into our everyday situations is where the foundation of trust is developed in our lives. Baby steps of obedience build spiritual authority. We can't trust the "almighty brain" or our gifts, even if God has given them to us. We don't throw our brains out, of course, but we *bring God into* our situations. As we do this, all of a sudden our brains work much better than they did before. It shouldn't amaze us that anointed revelation is so much wiser than our carnal reasoning. When we don't bring God into our everyday situations, fear rules in our hearts and we grow in doubt, not trust.

Trust is the foundation our faith is built upon. We should greatly desire to develop a more implicit trust and cultivate an attitude toward God that says, "This scares me to even think about this specific situation. But I choose to trust You. I believe You are available whether I feel You close to me or not." This is important because we can easily fail to trust God when we don't feel His presence as strongly as we would prefer.

Remember when Elijah ran from Jezebel and hid in a cave? God spoke to Elijah in a still, small voice, not in the wind, fire, or the earthquake that preceded it (see 1 Kings 19:11-12). God will rarely speak louder, so we must become quieter. He wants to train us to become sensitive to even the gentle whispers of His Spirit. The most significant spiritual equipping the Lord accomplishes in our life is His work of fine-tuning our spiritual sensitivity.

Even when we're not faithful, God still is. Taking matters into our own hands when we become afraid says to the Lord that we can do a better job than He can. Sometimes failure is our schooling in trust. It drives us back into the arms of God with greater humility and dependence. We must learn to depend on Him, put our trust in Him, and be confident that He will order our steps (see Prov. 3:1-4). The Lord invites us to give our worries and fears to Him because He cares for us (see 1 Pet. 5:7).

PRACTICAL APPLICATION

Let's get practical for a moment. Say your boss calls you on your way to work and tells you to bring the "x" files with you. Immediately you begin to fear because you don't know what he is talking about. In fact, you don't even know what the "x" files are, and you've surely never seen them. Probably the first feeling that accompanies those thoughts is a tension in your gut, followed by sudden panic. You have just lost your peace, but you don't have to lose it for the day. If you would just drop down and trust God, bringing Him into the situation, then your peace would return.

Suddenly, from that place of peace, you realize the "x" files are the "extra" files that the boss gave you the day before. You realize those extra files the boss was talking about are still sitting on your desk from the day before. Everything is going to be right with the world after all.

When I was a young Catholic boy, my mom taught me some bad theology. She discouraged me from "bothering" God with my prayers by telling me, "God is busy. Don't bother Him!" A better way to look at our interaction with God is to consider the joy of a mother when her little girl comes through the door with a flower in hand and rushes up to her mother to say, "I love you, Mommy!" However, if her young son ran up to her with a cut on his finger, his mother would respond with compassionate assistance. In both instances, love melts her heart. In the same way, it ravishes the heart of God when we rush to Him with *all* of our needs.

God doesn't get frustrated with us when we invite Him into these situations. He loves moving on our behalf and demonstrating the power of His peace. He is delighted when we trust Him and communicate with Him throughout the day, bringing Him into all of life. When we invite the Lord into these situations and then make decisions from the place of peace, suddenly we realize there is a much better way to live than being constantly stressed out and anxious.

When we trust God and welcome Him into each circumstance, words of wisdom come, insight comes, and revelations come because we choose to trust Him. For example, the transmission was acting up in our daughter's car, and we immediately thought it was going to cost hundreds of dollars. When I dropped down and wondered if I should stop by the auto store to get it looked at, I heard the Lord say, "Use a bottle of the 'red stuff.'" I didn't remember what it was called, but the last time I got the oil changed I had noticed a bottle of a red solution for the transmission for sale on a shelf. I went to the shop, purchased a bottle, poured it in...and the transmission worked perfectly. It appears that the red fluid sealed something vital in the lines. It demonstrates childlike trust when we welcome God into all the events of life—both large and small.

NO EXCUSES FOR NOT TRUSTING GOD

Trust is foundational for where God is taking the body of Christ. We only find it when we dive into intimacy with Him. One thing that plagues many in the church today is the fear of intimacy. But the truth is that all fruitfulness comes only from intimacy with God. Biblical fruitfulness flows from relationship with Him.

We know many people who have hidden for years behind theology and religious arguments that have separated them from intimacy with God. We have even heard some individuals condemn what they call "extra-biblical revelation," which is anything beyond simply reading the Bible. In other words, all we need is the written Word of God because that is the only way God speaks today. On the day of Pentecost, Peter said that the same Holy Spirit poured out on the early church is promised down through the generations (see Acts 2:38-39). God is *"the same yesterday, today, and forever"* (Heb. 13:8), so why would we have access to less of Him in the twenty-first century?

We cannot hide in our fears and fail to trust Christ because of religious arguments. The Pharisees were guilty of doing this in Jesus's time. Jesus said, *"You search the Scriptures, for in them you think you have eternal life; and these are they which testify of Me. But you are not willing to come to Me that you may have life"* (John 5:39-40). We only get life by coming *to* Him, not knowing something *about* Him.

We can distance ourselves from God and analyze what He is saying even with legitimate revelation. Thinking and talking about revelation do not change us. Revelation, like prophecy, points to potential. *Potential* means that we haven't done it yet. We receive the revelation and we get the interpretation, but then we have to apply it to our own personal life and walk it out with God. We cannot hide behind all of the gifts, rules, rituals, and spiritual traditions within our stream of Christianity.

We need to recognize what kind of fear is getting in the way when we are not trusting God. Was it something out of our control? When we are afraid, it is because we fear something happening that we don't want to happen or something not happening that we want to happen. Either way, who is in control of circumstances? God or us? Jesus says we shouldn't worry about our life for our heavenly Father knows what we need (see Matt. 6:25-34). If God watches over and feeds every tiny bird, how much more does He care about us? Every single one of our worries needs to be released into the hands of a loving God who has all the answers.

The lesson of *jurisdiction* is another vital principle for trusting God. We ministered a number of times at one particular church where the pastor used to tell me what to preach. My whole life before this I was used to going with the flow of the Holy Spirit. When God lays a message on my heart, that is the nugget with the most life for me and the most significance. But in this particular case, I needed to humble myself and trust God even if I had a different topic. That church wasn't my jurisdiction. As it turns out, I had some of the most powerful meetings I've ever had by doing that. God taught me a very important lesson about honoring those in authority.

At another time I was on a Pittsburgh television station, and they told me how many thousands of people were watching. The interviewer was asking me questions I wasn't interested in, and I didn't feel like I was flowing very well. So instead of answering the questions he asked, I just started speaking what I felt like God wanted me to say. Wow, did I get rebuked for that after the show.

The interviewer took me to the side room and told me that if I ever did something like that again, he would make sure I'd never get back on Christian television. I didn't know it at the time, but that was his area—his jurisdiction. God has the ability to have the interviewer ask the *right* questions—the questions *God* wants him or her to ask. I dropped down and released it all to God. So what if I felt like he was off and I was speaking for God? The Lord didn't appoint me to straighten the host out. God was asking me to trust Him. It's not about "being right." We can be right but be in the wrong spirit.

Comparing ourselves with others can also be disastrous in our growth in godliness; we must compare ourselves with God's standard for us. We need greater revelation of God as our peace. When we compete, compare, and covet, we forfeit contentment and enter into unhealthy rivalry with others. When we are content, we experience an inner enjoyment and acceptance of where we are in life. God has designed us to fit perfectly in the sphere to which He has assigned us. When we have an attitude like this, we can joyfully submit no matter what circumstances arise.

When we enter into rivalry with our brothers and sisters in Christ, it always interferes with the bond of peace in fellowship. God is the God of Peace. He has brought us to Himself through His shed blood, and He has broken down the dividing wall of hostility, making one man from the two, thus making peace (see Eph. 2:14-16). We must humble ourselves and agree with God, saying in our heart, "Lord, I want to honor You as the God of Peace. I want to include You in all relationships as well as every circumstance that I face."

STRESS ISN'T NECESSARY

At the end of the day, when the boss calls us into the office, our child's teacher calls us to say there's a problem at school, or we have car trouble on the road, we have to resist the tendency to get anxious and instead simply drop down in our hearts, letting the peace of God reign supreme. Many assume that stress is just a natural part of life. But with this we strongly disagree. We cannot be stressed and trust God at the same time.

We will face trouble and hardship in this world, but Jesus says that He has already overcome the world: *"I have told you these things, so that in Me you may have [perfect] peace and confidence. In the world you have tribulation and trials and distress and frustration; but be of good cheer [take courage; be confident, certain, undaunted]! For I have overcome the world. [I have deprived it of power to harm you and have conquered it for you]"* (John 16:33 AMP).

This overcoming Jesus is the One who gave us His own supernatural peace. If this peace is powerful enough for Jesus, it is certainly powerful enough for us. We must become proficient at including God in our daily life, letting the peace of God rule, and allowing God to transform the difficult situations we encounter. We don't have to live stressed-out lives.

Yes, there are always going to be stressful situations in this world. And we will partake of that stress whenever we fail to trust God and try to do things in our own strength. However, as we grow in our trust for God, peace invades our life and brings order where there was once chaos. We can all walk in greater peace than the church has ever imagined possible. In the last days, we will experience a powerful increase of peace like we've never known before.[5]

A LIFESTYLE STRATEGY
TO DE-STRESS

If stress is a problem in your life, here are some practical steps you can take to walk in more peace.

Prayer: Set aside a daily prayer time yielding to the presence of the Lord. This will acclimate you to His presence and allow you to practice yielding your will to the Lord. Isaiah said, *"Those who wait on the Lord shall renew their strength; they shall mount up with wings like eagles, they shall run and not be weary, they shall walk and not faint"* (Isa. 40:31).

Past: The undercurrent of unresolved and suppressed emotional baggage from the past can cause stress regardless of current life events.[6] Usually we allow God to bring issues to mind with no agenda of our own. However, we also encourage believers to spend a few months to specifically deal with past issues (such as mother, father, siblings, teachers, classmates, former pastors and church members, and so forth). Ask the Lord to reveal past and present issues contributing to your overall stress level. Spend a short time in prayer at the end of the day to deal with any unresolved situations so you don't carry today's trouble into tomorrow (see Eph. 4:26).

David prayed, *"Search me, O God, and know my heart; try me and know my anxious thoughts; and see if there be any hurtful way in me and lead me in the way everlasting"* (Ps. 139:23-24 NASB).

Present: Learn to deal quickly with the daily events of life. Anything that is not dealt with quickly is planted in the heart like a weed. Don't let it stay there and take root. If there is an overreaction to something, then take time to go to the Lord and ask Him to show you the root. If life pushes your buttons, you have the buttons in you! You can't change other people, but God can set you free. Paul reminds us, *"Don't stay angry. Don't go to bed angry. Don't give the devil that kind of foothold in your life"* (Eph. 4:26 MSG).

Peace: Emotions are friends who let you know you need to deal with something. Pay attention to any loss of peace. Notice when you feel anxiety and tension and deal with it quickly. Your peace will instantly return when you allow Christ the forgiver in you to forgive through you and/or release people and circumstances to God. Forgiveness cleanses the emotions and release gives control back to Him. *"Let the peace of God rule in your hearts"* (Col. 3:15).

Path: Practice walking in peace in everyday life, step by step. Whenever a stressful situation arises, release it back to the Lord. Every moment is a seed with potential for good when it is placed into the hands of God (see Rom. 8:28). Again, Paul reminds us, *"For shoes, put on the peace that comes from the Good News so that you will be fully prepared"* (Eph. 6:15 NLT).

TRUE TRANSFORMATION

The daily practice of the presence of God brings true change to our lives. We are changed from glory to glory as we behold the presence of God (see 2 Cor. 3:17-18). As we know Him for who He is, He transforms our character, nature, and motivation. His nature and character become engrafted within us as we behold the Person of God. When we draw close to Him in true intimacy, then our attitudes and the dispositions of our hearts become uncharacteristically optimistic.

Scientists have discovered that the emotion of love has some unique characteristics. In the natural, we feel love via a molecule of emotion called *oxytocin*. Molecules of emotion are neuropeptides, or "nerve proteins." When they connect with the receptors on the surface of our cell membranes, we interpret their signals as emotions. One of the special properties of oxytocin is that it causes change in both the brain and the emotional heart so the lives of two people can bond together in close relationship. Oxytocin is also a neuromodulator because it physically changes neurons and neural pathways in the brain itself.

Massive amounts of oxytocin are released when a baby is born, a man and woman fall in love, and when a person is born again. When we are born again, we are flooded with the love of God for the first time. Not only are we flooded with oxytocin, our emotions are also saturated with the supernatural glory of God's emotions. Every time we are in the presence of God, His love is transforming us. God begins to "mold us into the image of His Son":

For those whom He foreknew [of whom He was aware and loved beforehand], He also destined from the beginning...to be molded into the image of His Son [and share inwardly His likeness], that He might become the firstborn among many brethren (Romans 8:29 AMP).

Love changes us, transforming both the lover and the beloved. Oxytocin allows us to be transformed when we begin to see ourselves through the eyes of the one who loves us. Because of oxytocin, we can "unlearn" old perceptions and learn new ones. Love can "change our image of ourselves for the better, if we have an adoring partner."[7] This is true in human relationships, but how much more powerful when we begin to see ourselves through God's eyes.

Individuals are completely isolated from one another without relational bonds. Relational bonds are necessary or society could not exist. Oxytocin plus the fruit of the Spirit gives us the ability to open emotional doors and form close relationships in the realm of the Spirit. Christians have the astounding opportunity to form supernatural connections with God and other believers in the Spirit: *"And above all these [put on] love and enfold yourselves with the bond of perfectness [which binds everything together completely in ideal harmony]"* (Col. 3:14 AMP).

INTRINSIC VALUE

If we truly know we belong to God, we believe we have something of great value to give to others around us. He created us with intrinsic value. Gold and silver have intrinsic value no matter what form they take. They are valuable because of their essence. In the same way, we are valuable because we are created in the image and likeness of God. We have eternal worth. Our significance is derived from who we are, not from what we do. I can add nothing to my intrinsic value or subtract from it. Two other measures of value are determined by character and achievement, but nothing detracts from intrinsic value.

When we have an assurance of our intrinsic value, we begin to operate out of a place of intimacy. We don't try to gain the approval of God or other people but are rather motivated out of the approval we already have in God. We need to pursue greater consecration and sanctification, but we must start with a foundation of intimacy.

We may have spiritual gifts, a powerful anointing, and be used mightily by God. Some may even mistake this for His stamp of approval in our lives. But before Jesus ever did a single miracle, before He ever preached His first sermon, God opened up the heavens when He was baptized, expressing His delight in His Son: *"This is My beloved Son, in whom I am well pleased"* (Matt. 3:17).

Our gifting may increase with time. However, developing our gifts does not cause us to grow in God. Spiritual growth only happens as we yield ourselves to the God of all Peace, allowing Him to transform us into His image from one degree of glory to the next. We exhort you to learn to commune with God, and *"grow in the grace and knowledge of our Lord and Savior Jesus Christ"* (2 Pet. 3:18).

ENDNOTES

1. Charles Finney was a leading revivalist during the Second Great Awakening in America. He is well known for the anointing he carried as a result of being immersed in the Holy Spirit. Finney walked in such a strong sense of the presence of God that stories about him are legendary. "Finney seemed so anointed with the Holy Spirit that people were often brought under conviction of sin just by looking at him. When holding meetings at Utica, New York, he visited a large factory there and was looking at the machinery. At the sight of him one of the operatives, and then another, and then another broke down and wept under a sense of their sins, and finally so many were sobbing and weeping that the machinery had to be stopped while Finney pointed them to Christ." [J. G. Lawson, "Charles Finney: A Brief Biography," from *Deeper Experiences of Famous Christians*, (Anderson, IN: Warner Press; Abridged edition, 2007). Accessed May 7, 2014, at http://www.gospeltruth.net/lawsonbio.htm].

2. Several levels of faith are mentioned in the Scriptures. When Jesus beckoned Peter to get out of the boat and walk on the water, Peter's faith faltered and he began to sink beneath the waves. Jesus said to him, *"O you of little faith, why did you doubt?"* (Matt. 14:31). On the other hand, Jesus commended the centurion who believed He could simply speak a word and his servant would be healed, saying, *"Assuredly, I say to you, I have not found such great faith, not even in Israel!"* (Matt. 8:10).

3.   Walter Mischel, Ebbe B. Ebbesen, and Antonette Raskoff Zeiss (1972). "Cognitive and attentional mechanisms in delay of gratification," *Journal of Personality and Social Psychology*, 21 (2), 204–218.

4.   Jessie Penn-Lewis said that everyone wants to know the love of God and talk about the love of God. But we can't know the love of God until we know the God of truth. We have to receive Him before we can know Him. We have to trust before the love comes. We can beg God to experience His love, we can complain that we don't have the love of God in our lives, but we will never get the love of God in our hearts until we open up to Him and allow Him to come in and prove Himself. We are going to have to move into more implicit trust in God by receiving it.

5.   The truth about all of this is that practice makes permanent. Every one of us is responsible for our own spiritual growth. We can't blame God, the church, or anybody else for our problems. If we are to grow in the grace of God, then we must grow in trusting God, inviting Him into our life. As soon as we open our heart to trust Him, we sense His peace. No peace means no trust. When we make staying in peace a priority, we will automatically grow in both grace and trust.

Relationship is vital if we are to live a life that is saturated by the God of Peace. We can't just start anywhere on our Christian journey. We must start with the relationship first. We want to have a genuine relationship with the God of Peace. There is no substitute for intimacy, and it is what God prizes above all else.

To be qualified for the next move of God, we must know Him intimately. The determining factor will be whether or not we have the love and peace of God flowing out of us. Jesus had a stern warning for those who pursued gifts but neglected intimate relationship with Him:

> *Not everyone who says to Me, "Lord, Lord," shall enter the kingdom of heaven, but he who does the will of My Father in heaven. Many will say to Me in that day, "Lord, Lord, have we not prophesied in Your name, cast out demons in Your name, and done many wonders in Your name?" And then I will declare to them, "I never knew you; depart from Me, you who practice lawlessness!"* (Matthew 7:21-23)

To become intimate with God, we must spend time with Him in prayer. If we truly love someone, we want to spend time with that person. Failing to pray is in itself an attitude of dishonor.

In our time of prayer, we should always approach the Lord with honor: "God, I'm here to honor You. I don't want to grieve or resist You. I yield to Your peace. I want to know You as my peace. I yield to a more implicit trust in You so Your peace will rule in my heart and in all my interactions. I welcome You into all of the events of today. When I forget to yield to the Holy Spirit, I pray that You would remind me to include You."

6. The first year we were married, I (Jen) came home from work one day complaining about an ongoing situation that

was stressful for me. When I explained what was going on, Dennis told me I was overreacting. He asked me to close my eyes and ask the Lord for the root issue. Much to my surprise, an incident from a childhood experience at school came to mind in which I had been frustrated with the demands of a particular teacher. I forgave my teacher. The next day, lo and behold, the individual with whom I had been frustrated was no longer an issue. I had peace instead of stress. My own unresolved emotions from the past had been creating stress in the present. Regardless of the circumstances of life, unresolved emotional issues can create added stress.

7.   N. Doidge, *The Brain That Changes Itself* (New York: Penguin Group (USA), Inc., 2007), 118-121.

CHAPTER 12

THE FIVE GS OF PSALM 23

BY DENNIS

THE ROCK OF GOD

Jen and I pastor a church called Kingdom Life Church in South Carolina. Not only do we have a local congregation that we minister to, but we also stream most of our services live over the Internet. And those who wish to do so can go back through the archives and watch past services we've done over several months.

A couple living in Minnesota, Karl and Amelia, regularly watch our Internet services. Amelia sent us a testimony not too long ago that confirms a lot of what we've been teaching. She had watched a service we did a week prior, and then she wrote to us to share just a little bit of what took place within her.

She said that I prayed at the end of the message for those who were watching via the Internet. I prayed through the steps to release circumstances and the fear of the unknown. So she entered into the prayer and released her thoughts and her own ideas on where to live, issues with finances, the kids, and schooling, as these were all up in the air for them at the moment. She was instantly flooded with the peace of God as she did this.

Suddenly, however, she felt a strong weightiness in her spirit. When she was wondering if she had lost her peace, she heard me start to talk about how God was revealing Himself to people as a rock, and that some would begin to feel Christ the rock in their spirit. It was a confirmation that what she was doing and the decisions she was making were from the Lord.

The first time Jen and I experienced Christ the rock was during the time when we were moving into a new house and selling our old one. The house inspector had just found a number of issues that we needed to correct and we were scrambling to take care of everything necessary before closing on the house. So much was going on with one minor crisis right after another that it was difficult to stay in a flow of peace. In the midst of all this, one day we pulled up in front of the old house and suddenly felt a strong sense of stability inside and out. As we looked around, we could feel a tangible steadiness of the God who is in control of all circumstances. After this experience, it was even easier to stay in peace no matter what.

Some of the revelation that God has been giving us during our devotional time verifies this as well. God wants to confirm what He has been speaking to all of us, that we are on the right track and we are not to deviate from it. In fact, God calls us to stay the course in whatever direction He is revealing to us at the moment. As we focus on where God is confirming His will, fruit will be produced in our lives.

We can obey God without knowing all the facts in life or what is down the road, but it is obedience nonetheless. God shines His light on the next step then the one after that. We walk in the light that we have. It is important we stay the course in whatever direction God is guiding us at the present moment.

Once when I was mentoring an intellectually brilliant young man, he became frustrated that his spiritual progress proceeded at a much slower pace than his academic pursuits. He later gave me a Bible as a gift and wrote: "To Dennis, who taught me that the education of the mind comes through much study, but the education of the heart comes only by the anointing of God." This was very perceptive. The Lord focuses on one area at a time until it becomes second nature to us. Often, if you are not hearing anything from the Lord, take a look at your journal and see if you acted on the last thing He revealed to you. Be obedient to that and He will give you more.

> *Therefore take heed how you hear. For whoever has, to him more will be given; and whoever does not have, even what he seems to have will be taken from him* (Luke 8:18).

AN INFINITE DIAMOND

God can be likened to an infinite diamond with inexhaustible facets and endless depths to every facet. The metaphor of the diamond is perfect for understanding our pursuit to know God more intimately. Every additional aspect of knowing God causes our Christianity to become deeper, so our Christian life begins to really work, and we begin walking in the actual substance of that relationship.

When we walk in a specific facet of Christ for a prolonged period of time, it then proves to be a strength in our life, which is where fruitfulness comes in. God wants to show Himself faithful in many different arenas of life, displaying His character and nature. It is His desire that we move into relationship with Him in each of those areas, whether that is peace, faith, hope, courage, or whatever else God may be revealing at the moment. Jesus Christ is the rock upon whom we are to build our lives, where He shows up experientially for us. And it is out of this rock that rivers of water flow (see Ps. 78:16).

We must not build our faith on the sand of theoretical knowledge, but on the bedrock of an experiential faith. Of course, we don't want to have an experience with God for the sake of experience alone. God reveals Himself to us so that we can enter into more reality of Him. It is an invitation to receive His nature. God becomes more and more real to us. It was never God's intention that we would only know *about* Him but that we would become more intimately acquainted with Him in the depths of knowledge.

FIVE-FOLD MINISTRY OF PEACE IN PSALM 23

God has been speaking to us for a number of years about the five-fold ministry of peace through which He guides, governs, gathers, guards, and grounds us in His peace. There are many different aspects of His peace that we can enter into. Just as the five-fold ministry of the apostle, prophet, evangelist, pastor, and teacher was emphasized progressively from the '70s to the '90s, so God is now emphasizing the wonders of the ministry of peace using the five Gs.

When we cooperate with the lordship of Jesus Christ, we begin to see His peace manifested in all that we do. As He sets up His government of peace within us, we will have more peace in our guidance, we will have more peace in the sense of being guarded, and we will have more peace in our relationships with others. In fact, we will have more peace in all of our circumstances, knowing that His peace is militant and establishes dominion.

During our prayer time one morning, Jen received a powerful revelation of the five Gs of peace contained in Psalm 23. She didn't even have to study it for hours to fully understand what God was speaking through it. It just came as she was praying one morning, and God downloaded it into her spirit in a matter of minutes. She opened up the Bible and saw it so clearly.

> *The Lord is my shepherd; I shall not want. He makes me to lie down in green pastures; He leads me beside the still waters. He restores my soul; He leads me in the paths of righteousness for His name's sake. Yea, though I walk through the valley of the shadow of death, I will fear no evil; for You are with me; Your rod and Your staff, they comfort me. You prepare a table before me in the presence of my enemies; You anoint my head with oil; my cup runs over. Surely goodness and mercy shall follow me all the days of my life; and I will dwell in the house of the Lord forever* (Psalm 23:1-6).

Govern

David begins by saying, *"The Lord is my shepherd; I shall not want..."* (Ps. 23:1). Psalm 23 begins with a revelation of lordship. When Jesus is truly Lord of our life, He is in control of all things. He governs our life. We can fully submit ourselves to Him and know Him as our Shepherd. Did you know that sheep are the only grazing animals that need the continual care of a shepherd? We can't be trusted to fend for ourselves.

Because God is the Good Shepherd and we are the sheep of His pasture, understanding this relationship is important to our walk in the peace of God. If He is our Shepherd, then we must learn to be obedient sheep. We must learn to trust Him even when we don't have all the answers. As a Shepherd, He is constantly governing us in all of our interactions throughout the day.

When Jen first began to talk about this in our prayer time, I really began to consider how we are prone to wander. The old song really is true:

> *Prone to wander, Lord, I feel it,*
> *Prone to leave the God I love.*[1]

Most sheep have a tendency to separate from the flock and go astray. In spite of hearts that too often tend to wander, God reveals Himself as the Good Shepherd who lovingly corrals us. If we do roam away for a moment, it is easy to just receive forgiveness, saying in our heart, "God, I receive Your forgiveness for wandering." Once we do that, peace will be restored.

One of the important values of our church is freedom in the Spirit. Gifts and creativity flourish in an atmosphere of freedom but freedom must be balanced with responsibility and obedience. There is a way to walk in freedom without letting our hearts go astray. As we develop our relationship with God, therefore, we realize there are fences that the Lord has made, not to restrict us but to protect us. He has given us boundaries that we are to stay within. They are not to confine freedom, but they are to cultivate it.

Jen and I have an a deck on our two-story house that looks out over our backyard. Jen still doesn't like to stand too close to the railing because it is high off the ground. Heights don't bother me, so I love to stand there and just look out at the landscape and trees. But I only enjoy standing there because there is a railing between me and the ground below. I wouldn't enjoy it nearly as much if there wasn't the safety of the railing present. It provides comfort for me so I can actually enjoy the view. It is not restriction or a confinement, and it is surely not a limitation. It actually allows us to enjoy our home much more.

The fact that David says *"I shall not want"* is significant here. If we really believe that God is absolutely, 100 percent good, then we can nullify an insidious tactic of the enemy. He tries to tell us that we're somehow being limited and cheated in life. It's as old as the lie that was first told in the Garden of Eden, "Did God really say that you could have everything but *this*?" Sheep go astray because they think they are being limited in some way. But God is a Good Shepherd who sets up healthy boundaries so that we can thrive and enjoy what He has made.

In the place where God's peace governs, there we will not lack any good thing.

Guide

Next, guidance is clearly evident throughout this psalm. David says of the Lord, *"He makes me to lie down in green pastures; He leads me beside the still waters. He restores my soul; He leads me in the paths of righteousness for His name's sake"* (Ps. 23:2-3). Another way to translate "still waters" is *peaceful streams.* The first place the Lord brings us is to green pastures and the river of His peace. Green pastures represent life and provision.

Sheep will not rest unless they feel secure and their hunger and thirst are satisfied. Because God is good, He will always lead us to green pastures and sit beside still waters. When we are yielded and obedient to the presence of God within, He will cause us to enter His rest. *"Therefore, since a promise remains of entering His rest, let us fear lest any of you seem to have come short of it"* (Heb. 4:1).

We believe the days are coming when the church will enter a rest like we've never known before. The rest of faith has been sorely missing in the church, and we've accepted stress as the normal way of life. Stress is *not* normal for Christians. God is inviting us to enter into Him, the God of Peace, and find rest. God also taught David to yield his heart in obedience and child-like trust. Our soul is restored as we allow God to govern more and more of our heart.

Not only does God bring us to the place of rest, but He actually leads us in the paths of righteousness as well. Righteous acts are those prompted by God and done in a flow of love and peace. When peace guides our hearts and minds, He will lead us in ways that bring righteousness to us and those around us.

God guides us in our decision making by His peace. Isaiah confirms this when he says, *"Your ears shall hear a word behind you, saying, 'This is the way, walk in it,' whenever you turn to the right hand or whenever you turn to the left"* (Isa. 30:21).

Ground

The word "ground" is *themelioo* in the Greek, meaning "to lay a foundation" (see Eph. 3:17). The peace of God grounds us in the nature and character of God. When David mentioned that God restores his soul, he was speaking of the process of sanctification taking place within him. God healed David's heart, setting him free from all the wounds he had previously experienced.

God always leads us in order to ground us. The Lord wants to teach us the ways of peace so we will be *"holy and blameless... in His sight"* and *"continue in the faith, grounded and steadfast"* (Col. 1:22-23). The only way we can learn to walk the path of peace is by practice. For us to become grounded in Him, we must walk in peace in daily life. In the process of learning peace, we grow in our relationship with God. A sheep learns to follow of his shepherd but will flee from the voice of a stranger (see John 10:4-5).

If we don't understand that God grounds us in His peace, healing our heart and filling our emotions with the fruit of the Spirit, then we will have difficulty entering into the fullness of what He has for us in these days. God's kingdom of peace must come and displace all of the pain, anxiety, and worry that so often brings torment. He grounds us in His nature, in the infinite facets of who He is. As the Good Shepherd leads us and guides us in paths of righteousness, we get established and built up in Him. As the Lord becomes the foundation of our life, we become stable and secure in Him.

Guard

David continues, *"Yea, though I walk through the valley of the shadow of death, I will fear no evil; for You are with me; Your rod and Your staff, they comfort me"* (Ps. 23:4).

Sheep become very vulnerable when they face danger. At times the shepherd must lead his flock through mountainous terrain with deep ravines and gulches to find better pastureland and shelter from inclement weather. Predators crouch amongst the boulders and flash floods are commonplace. They truly are in the valley of the shadow of death.

The sheep, of course, are often oblivious to the dangers all around them, but the shepherd is all too aware. Sometimes our Shepherd guides us through the trials of life, and we come out on the other side with a testimony of His love and care. But how many times has the Lord saved us from perils about which we were completely ignorant? When God is the Shepherd who guards us, we can walk through very difficult circumstances and know that He is with us even in the midst of the tremendous turmoil.

God's rod and His staff comfort us. The rod defends the sheep from danger, but the staff is used for gentle care and kindness. His staff uniquely identifies a shepherd, and it is made especially for working with sheep. Only a shepherd uses a staff. The staff helps guide the sheep when they wander and draws them back close to their shepherd. Often, the shepherd will gently nudge a reluctant sheep to stay on the path or walk through a narrow passageway. When a sheep gets tangled in briars, the staff is used to gently pull them free.

The rod is used as protection from wolves and other dangerous predators such as coyotes or wild dogs. It is a symbol of authority, strength, and power. The shepherd uses his rod as a weapon to drive wild beasts away from the sheep. Knowing that God guards us should bring tremendous comfort to our hearts, because we know that He is continuously protecting us. Even when we sleep, the Lord watches over us. He's the Good Shepherd who guards the sheep from those who seek their harm.

Go and Gather

"You prepare a table before me in the presence of my enemies; You anoint my head with oil; my cup runs over" (Ps. 23:5). As God governs, guides, grounds, and guards us, then our cup begins to overflow. And it is out of this overflow, springing up out of our intimate relationship with God, that we are prepared to share the good news of peace with all those around us.

> *How beautiful upon the mountains are the feet of him who brings good news, who proclaims peace, who brings glad tidings of good things, who proclaims salvation, who says to Zion, "Your God reigns!"* (Isaiah 52:7)

We become equipped for the role of the evangelist, where we go to those who do not believe and gather those who already do. The magnetic pull of the peace of God rules and reigns in our hearts. It is from this fullness that we minister.

Real ministry is not our gift, our talent, or our cleverness. Real ministry is ministering out of the overflow of what Christ has ministered to us. If we don't have a time of private ministry in the presence of God, then we are not going to have much of a public one.

When our cup overflows, however, we're ready to go and gather with the peace of God. God is giving us a sense of God-confidence so we can go into the marketplace where the peace of God will have magnetic drawing power.

God is wooing us to the mountain of the Lord and knitting us together with others in the body of Christ, which is a corporate knitting of hearts. We are coming together in unity, as described in Psalm 133. When we are rightly connected with Christ, our Head, and one another, we are candidates for the oil of refreshing, the oil that runs down from Aaron's head, flowing down to the hem of his garments.

Goodness and mercy will follow us all the days of our lives (see Ps. 23:6). The word *follow* is the Hebrew word *radaf*, which actually means to pursue. This means that God's goodness and mercy will pursue us all the days of our lives. We can never escape being overtaken by His goodness, extravagant generosity, and mercy. His unfailing love is expressed through His kindness, tenderness, and faithfulness.

When we first begin to participate in church life, each of us must discover our identity in Christ and develop our individual gifts and callings. It doesn't stop there, however. God plants us in church families to learn interdependence. In community, we become part of a family mission, the purpose for which God has drawn us together as a congregation. Working as one, our corporate identity and corporate gifts and callings can emerge.

God is calling us to move beyond false independence, which only emphasizes what we can do individually, to interdependence, or true community. The spiritual connection that defines godly interdependence is the bond of peace. It begins with heart knittings and culminates in one accord. The word *bond* is *sundesmos* in the Greek, meaning that which binds together, or "ligaments which bind the bones of a body together." Bones that are disconnected from one another cannot move or function. *Bond* is also figuratively used for the bands that unite the body of Christ (see Eph. 4:3).

While it is true that there is a mystical worldwide body of Christ, God also desires that the hearts of believers be knit together in real-life loving relationships bound together in true biblical unity. In such unity, a congregation can function as a *living organism* with its life source—the supernatural life of the Spirit of God. Members of a fellowship of believers who are joined together in heart and spirit can function harmoniously in the power of the Spirit. Our Shepherd says His sheep will hear His voice and *there will be one flock and one shepherd* (John 10:16).

Even though, in the flesh, we may not want to be "fenced in," God is drawing us to healthy interdependence. Why? Because God wants a home to dwell in with His family—the Shepherd dwelling with His sheep. W. P. Keller comments:

> [The shepherd] has taken us from the green pastures and still waters of the home ranch, up through the mountain passes onto the high tablelands of the summer range. Fall has come with its storms and rain

and sleet that drives the sheep down to the foothills
and back to the home ranch for the long, quiet winter.
In a sense this is coming home.[2]

Psalms 23:6 concludes with the longing of David's heart: *"And I will dwell in the house of the Lord forever."* Between verses 5 and 6, Psalm 23 has a shift of imagery from the sheep with his Shepherd to David as an esteemed guest in the house of the Lord. Prior to verse 5, Psalm 23 tells of the sheep who know the care of the Lord, but here David is lifted up to dwell forever in the extravagant riches of the King's abode. The prayers of the shepherd boy who desired nothing more than living in the presence of God are answered (see Rev. 3:12).

It is the longing of the heart of God that we live in His presence. The Lord has searched for a dwelling place since the time of creation, a place where He could dwell in the midst of His people (see Eph. 2:22). And what will permit this to happen? Interdependence and unity as defined by God.

The peace of God comes to govern, guide, guard, gather, and ground us in who He is and what He has done for us. God invites us to go deeper with Him as we walk in more and more of His peace.

Going Deeper

God always reveals Himself to us in many different ways. Not only does He reveal many different expressions of Himself, but there are depths to each of those facets that take us into deeper and deeper experiences with the Lord. We can always go deeper in our relationship with God. We will never plumb the depths of His presence or cease to wonder at His riches as mentioned previously.

When I was a young Christian, I would experience God in specific ways for a certain length of time. Once I was grounded in what God was revealing to me, He would then take me into a new experience of a different facet of Himself. I would focus on soaking in His love for a season. Next, He would teach me a new lesson in experiencing His peace. Each time, revelation became reality and reality found practical expression in my life.

With each revelation, God was laying a deeper foundation of His character and divine nature within me. It would seem that God would continually take me in a circle, always bringing me back around to something He had revealed sometimes years prior. This wasn't because I lost the revelation of Him as my peace but because He wanted to take me *deeper* into the realm of peace. I learned to trust Him in different ways, and He drew me deeper and deeper into each revelation He gave. God doesn't reveal Himself because we forgot what He was like, but so we can experience greater depths of His character and nature.

God wants us to know each particular facet so it becomes a part of our life. His nature must become our nature as well. When God reveals Himself as the God of Peace, He wants us to experience Him in such a way that His peace becomes ours. That way when God reveals Himself in another way down the road, we are operating often unconsciously from a greater place of peace. Then it may be that God will bring us back around to the revelation of the God of Peace in another year or two. He is only adding to the richness of the depths of Christ.

We pray that the revelation of the God of Peace would become more real to you in the days ahead. We believe there is a great breakthrough of supernatural peace coming to the body of Christ, whereby we will walk in the power of peace in a real and authentic way. This peace is not passive or lazy, but militaristic and full of authority. And it is the government of His peace that God is establishing within us.

The Lord is drawing us to Himself so we can experience a profoundly renewed peace deep within us, an assurance that God is the rock upon which our foundation is built. Our relationship with Him must move to a level of intimacy in which our will becomes one with His will—a romance of the wills. Only through our obedience can we come closer to God. Jesus said:

> He who has My commandments and keeps them, it is he who loves Me. And he who loves Me will be loved by My Father, and I will love him and manifest Myself to him (John 14:21).

The prophet Ezekiel was a seer of visions who had been carried away captive to Babylon. The Book of Ezekiel begins with a vision of God that set his heart on fire with the nature and glory of God. In Ezekiel 37:22-28, he speaks of the restored Tabernacle of David—the people of God with the presence of God in their midst. This is followed by his visions of a new city and a new temple filled with the glory of God (see Ezek. 43:1-7).

The Spirit brought him to the door of the temple, and he beheld a wondrous sight. Water bubbled up from within the temple and flowed forth from the threshold of the eastern gate. By the description of the properties of this water, this was living water, reminiscent of the rivers that watered the Garden of Eden (see Gen. 2:10-14). The river brought forth life, abundance, and healing. The trees that grew along the banks abounded with fruit for food and leaves for healing (see Ezek. 47:7-9). Surely this was none other than the living water in the final chapter in the Book of Revelation (see Rev. 22:1-2)!

The tale of the kingdom of God on earth began in the Garden of Eden—God dwelling with His children. It is not just a story from long ago. This is still a promise for us today. The seven messages to the churches in the Book of Revelation contain promises for those who overcome and enter the realm of the kingdom. Included in the seven promises is the promise of the restoration of all that was forfeited in Eden. Hear what the Spirit says to us, *"He who has an ear, let him hear what the Spirit says to the churches. To him who overcomes I will give to eat from the tree of life, which is in the midst of the Paradise of God"* (Rev. 2:7). We have been granted access to the very Garden forfeited by Adam and Eve. It is time to claim our inheritance!

We know that all believers receive the Holy Spirit at the time of salvation, but God has so much more in store for us. God wants us to be transfigured in His presence and filled with His fullness. Paul prayed God would grant us exactly that:

> *For this reason I bow my knees to the Father of our Lord Jesus Christ, from whom the whole family in heaven and earth is named, that He would grant you, according to the riches of His glory, to be strengthened with might through His Spirit in the inner man, that Christ may dwell in your hearts through*

faith; that you, being rooted and grounded in love, may be able to comprehend with all the saints what is the width and length and depth and height—to know the love of Christ which passes knowledge; that you may be filled with all the fullness of God. Now to Him who is able to do exceedingly abundantly above all that we ask or think, according to the power that works in us, to Him be glory in the church by Christ Jesus to all generations, forever and ever. Amen (Ephesians 3:14-21).

We have not yet entered into the wondrous things God has clearly prepared for us. At this time, it is apparent that a rivulet, not a mighty river, is flowing from our churches. He must have more of us before we have more of Him. Our responsibility is to yield to His lordship.

Ezekiel described different depths of the river—to the ankles, to the knees, to the waist, and finally a river that could not be crossed because the water was so deep. It was water in which one must swim. When we wade in shallow water or even waist-deep water, we are still able to move on our own. Our will can still exert itself quite easily.

However, in the deep water of the Spirit of God, He moves us as *He* wishes. As we enthrone God in our lives, we begin to experience the mighty river that flows from His throne. We yield to Him. He is in control. We become yielded vessels who rest in God and move only according to the flow of His will. The more we rest, the deeper our peace becomes. The cry of our heart becomes the cry of God's heart: *"Thy kingdom come. Thy will be done in earth, as it is in heaven"* (Matt. 6:10 KJV).

We pray that this Scripture would become a reality to you as you pursue the God of all Peace:

> *[For my determined purpose is] that I may know Him [that I may progressively become more deeply and intimately acquainted with Him, perceiving and recognizing and understanding the wonders of His Person more strongly and more clearly], and that I may in that same way come to know the power outflowing from His resurrection* (Philippians 3:10 AMP).

ENDNOTES

1. "Come, Thou Fount of Every Blessing," written by Robert Robinson in 1757. Public domain.

2. W.P. Keller, *A Shepherd Looks at Psalm 23*, (Grand Rapids, MI: Zondervan, 2007), 137.

ABOUT THE CLARKS

Dennis and Dr. Jen equip believers to heal themselves, then to facilitate healing to others. It is not counseling in the traditional sense, but a brand-new approach, teaching believers how to experience the peace of God in everyday life, and how to deal quickly and completely with anything interrupting their peace. Some individuals may just want to receive quick healing for a few wounds and traumas, but many others have become committed to making peace a way of life, like the Clarks have learned to do.

They have spent years developing teaching materials based on spiritual revelation that has now been developed into targeted training modules which can be tailored for mature believers, new converts, Sunday school teachers, youth pastors, church discipleship programs, pastoral care, restoration, ministry teams, missionaries, and lay workers. The simple keys are easy enough for a mother or Sunday school worker to teach a 3-year-old child, yet effective enough to heal the deepest hurts of adults quickly and completely. Advanced topics are also taught in other training seminars: dealing with the thought life, emotional health, willpower, addiction, deliverance, sexual issues, physical healing, and spiritual discernment.

Dennis and Dr. Jen are the authors of *Deep Relief Now, Live Free: Discover the Keys to Living in God's Presence 24/7, Deep Relief Now: Simple Keys for Quickly Healing Your Longstanding Emotional Pain*. In addition, they have a series for children, *The Great God Quest*, that teaches the how-tos to children. Dr Jen is also author of *Was Jesus a Capitalist?*

clark@forgive123.com

www.forgive123.com